D0935619

English
Renaissance
Literature

Introductory Lectures

Frank Kermode
Stephen Fender
Kenneth Palmer

Gray-Mills Publishing
10 Juer Street, London SW11

First edition 1974

Frank Kermode, Stephen Fender, Kenneth Palmer

SBN 85641 022 5 (cloth)
SBN 85641 023 3 (paper)

Printed in Great Britain by
Lowe & Brydone (Printers) Ltd.,
London and Thetford

CONTENTS

PREFACE

This collection makes no pretence of being anything more than it seems. It is a record of part of the teaching done in one literature course in one college over a period of six months. The teachers concerned have all written about their special interests, and appear in this book in quite a different role; as oral performers in lectures and seminars.

The lecture is a peculiar institution, and people have often said they can't see why it survived the invention of printing. Virginia Woolf ridiculed the universities for their adherence to this obsolete form, and J. B. Trapp, in *Background to the English Renaissance* (Gray-Mills), points out that the same criticism was made in the sixteenth century. And it was true that the lecture (which means, etymologically, "reading") was invented in order to communicate and comment on the contents of manuscript books not available to students. In a time when books and commentaries are all too abundant, why have lectures at all? And although this criticism neglects the well-known truth that institutions may remain valuable long after the disappearance of their immediate cause, some answer is required.

The utilitarian answer, that people find it easier to be told things than to find out for themselves, is at best a bit shabby; furthermore, it is probably untrue. There remain three good reasons for lecturing. The first, that new information can still, in certain circumstances, be best conveyed by a (perhaps illustrated) oral communication, and discussed there and then, is operative at a higher level than we are here contemplating. The second is that an experienced lecturer, working with skeleton notes, and thinking on his feet, quite often says things that had never before precisely occurred to him — which is exciting both for him and his auditors. The third answer also has to do with excitement; a good lecture can be highly affective, fill students with an immediate enthusiasm, send them to books and start them thinking.

Naturally many lectures fall short of this ideal, and nobody would any longer dream of depending on them in the old way. The seminar, in which a group of eight or ten students discuss the material with a teacher, is perhaps more important, though even more transient, more purely oral, than the lecture; and the tutorial, one teacher and one student talking, may be the most private, indescribable and valuable of all forms of study.

In this course we used all these modes of teaching, but the present book reproduces only some of the lectures on the principal authors. One wing of the course, which dealt with minor literature of the period, we have had unfortunately to omit. So what follows consists of a selection from routine lectures given between October 1972 and March 1973.

It's important to stress that they *are* purely routine. Nobody put on a special show, and the editing of the transcripts has been minimal. What you will read here is not what the authors would have *written*; it is what they happened to *say* at a particular moment, when thinking about Spenser or Donne or Milton. Much of what they say has been said before (though a little, as it happens, is new). All of it has been re-thought and given impromptu expression. It was suggested to us, and rightly or wrongly we have agreed, that such a record would be of interest and assistance to other students of the subject, who might even feel more at ease with the rough colloquial texture than with the smoothness of a more formal text-book.

Frank Kermode.

I

POLITICAL AND ECCLESIASTICAL ALLEGORY IN *THE FAERIE QUEENE*

FRANK KERMODE

It is important to understand the concept of the epic in the Renaissance and how an inheritance from Virgil would necessarily require the epic to have a political dimension. This would entail in its turn all the things you would find in Spenser; many varieties of imagery, and interest in matters other than politics — in ethics, for example, and theology — but above all it would entail a very strange version of history. If you think of Virgil proclaiming, in the 6th Book of the *Aeneid*, the imperial future of Rome, you have a very grand central image of what different Renaissance nations felt that they had to do when they began to feel their nationality very strongly. Nationalism in the Renaissance replaces the universalism of the Middle Ages: the idea of Europe, or of the whole Christian world, as united and belonging to an empire which descended from the Roman Empire in the form of the Holy Roman Empire, crumbled. The quarrels between the Emperor and the Pope were inherited with the religious disputes of the Renaissance; hence all the debates about the relationship between the head of the State and the head of the Church. This was solved in England by Henry VIII, who made himself head of both. Elizabeth had to consolidate that and we still, in a rather feeble way, maintain this tradition.

This is the Renaissance solution, the nationalist solution, to a very old argument — just as the argument as to whether nationality was important in itself goes right back to Dante. Once you have a nation and a language — and that's another thing — you have to give your language the prestige and power of Latin, which is the "natural" language for a universalist organisation. You require poems which, in the vernacular, do for the history of a nation what the *Aeneid* did for Rome. Everybody, really, had a go at this. The epic was the great Renaissance form. Very few people at that time would have thought of saying that tragedy was a higher form than the epic, because epic had within it the potential of satisfying this kind of requirement; this need to give to the language, and the people who spoke it, the sort of strength and vigour, with its roots in the past, that Rome had established through Virgil.

The history they recount is not at all like anything we would recognise as a history of England. That's the first thing one has got to realize, I think, in considering the political aspects of Spenser's epic. You have to learn a new version of history. You have to see English history as it was convenient to see it in 1590. You also have to remember that political and ecclesiastical history were really one and the same thing. They were not two separate subjects. So the history of England tends, to a very great extent, to be written as a history of the Church.

Once you accept that, and are prepared to learn a whole new nonsensical sort of history, you'll find a lot of things fall into place in the *Faerie Queene*. There are two articles that you ought to read if you possibly can. These are two of the most important articles ever written which have a bearing on Spenser, but neither of them has been collected in any book so you have to go to the original sources for them. One of them is by Frances Yates and it is called "Queen Elizabeth as Astraea." It's a very long article of about 70 pages and it is published in the *Journal of the Warburg and Courtauld Institutes (JWCI)* Vol. X, 1947. The other is by a pupil of Frances Yates, Roy Strong. It is called "The Popular Celebration of the Accession Day of Queen Elizabeth I" and that appeared in *JWCI* Vol. XXI, 1958. Both these articles are immensely illuminating. I'll be referring to them as I go along.

This strange, propagandist history — because that's what it is, for Elizabethan historians rewrote their history as ruthlessly as any totalitarian regime of modern times — is clearly seen in the key work, Foxe's *Book of Martyrs*, as it is called. Its real name is Foxe's *Actes and Monuments* and it was published in 1563. It's a huge book, really a sort of history of the world, a history of everything, but especially of England. It was so important that every church had to have a copy, as well as the Bible, and it was even chained up like the Bible. Nowadays we tend to get it in abridged versions, but it is an absolutely enormous book. Of course it has very little to do with history as we understand it.

Such works were highly important for Elizabeth, who had a very shaky start with a not very secure claim to the throne and a very tricky ecclesiastical situation. The country had just emerged from a Catholic reign. It was very important for her to have scholars and propagandists to make her claim seem valid, to make, in fact, the Church Settlement seem valid. Foxe was therefore a great success.

Bishop Jewel was also successful in 1562 with a work called *Apologia Ecclesiae Anglicanae*, which was translated at the time as *An Apology for the English Church*. A few years later, in 1572, Archbishop Parker wrote a book called *De Antiquitate Britanniae Ecclesiae* about the antiquity of the British Church.

Now all these books really do the same thing, though not quite in the same way (Foxe was the most popular). They argue that the true Church was founded in England by Joseph of Arimathea immediately after the crucifixion; that the Roman Church is a late upstart; and that the history of England, after the "good" years, is a sell-out to Rome, reaching its depths in the eleventh century, when Gregory VII was the great Pope, and took over, with the aid of the Norman Kings, the independent Church of England. We remained in that captivity from the eleventh to the fourteenth century, when Wyclif, and stirrings of English reformation, appeared. The importance of this, as you see, is to represent the English reformation not as something new but as a reversion to something older and purer than the Roman Church.

Elizabeth came to be celebrated as the Queen who restored that ancient, pristine purity to the Church: not just the Church of England, but to the Catholic Church as a whole. For that reason she was represented as Astraea, the Goddess of Justice and Equity, who had left the world when the decline began, when the Golden Age ended; Elizabeth was Astraea returned, as Virgil had prophesied in the famous *Fourth Eclogue*. Elizabeth, therefore, *was* Astraea. She was also the true Church, the bride of the Song of Songs, of the Book of Revelation, and almost anything else you can think of that would enhance her historical and ecclesiastical dignity. It was also very convenient, of course, that Astraea was also called Virgo — *iam redit et Virgo*, now the Virgin returns, is Virgil's tag — and so this became part of the cult of Elizabeth's virginity also. She represented the true union of Christ and his Church; almost, in a sense, the end of time. This is all very blasphemous, one might think. But it didn't seem so at the time. All these things were celebrated — as you will see in Roy Strong's article. They weren't bizarre things, done by a few cultists at the Court; they happened in the great holiday, the second in importance after Christmas, of the Queen's accession day. All the popular celebrations reflected these themes. Roy Strong shows that Elizabeth was represented not only as Astraea, but with all this other imagery attached to her. She grew more and more like the Virgin

Mary, so that after her death and well on into the reign of James I, she was still being painted as something like the Virgin Mary and apparently being used for devotional purposes. It is a very strange and interesting story.

The importance for Spenser is that this purely legendary history of the conflicts between the true English and the false Roman Church are in evidence, particularly in the first Book. There is a tradition, for example, of Popes who were not only very wicked but who were magicians of one sort or another. Gregory VII had this reputation, as did Sylvester II, and there were others who were very like Archimago who is clearly meant to be a kind of wicked magician/Pope figure. There are many allusions, which I'll point out shortly, to this anti-Romanist history. It is a history, incidentally — and this should be stressed — which is basically founded upon interpretations of the Book of Revelation. The Book of Revelation was taken — not by everyone, but particularly by Protestants — as the key to history, as predicting the Reformation. This was so, not only for English theologians but for theologians all over the Continent.

The Pope fits into this Anti-Christ, who actually doesn't appear in the Book of Revelation, curiously enough, but became identified with the Beast from the Land, who has to be slaughtered by the Knight faithful and true, in a kind of chivalric battle, before Christ can harrow Hell and bring time to an end. All this is built into Book I of the *Faerie Queene.*

If you bear this kind of pattern in mind when you think of Book I you can see how very undreamy this allegedly rather dreamy poet actually was. There are elements of real, hard propaganda in the *Faerie Queene* which fed an appetite that already existed. It's the nature of that appetite, I think, that makes it important for you to look at these details as they're spelt out by Frances Yates and Roy Strong.

If you look at cantos i and ii of Book I in the light of these facts, then I think you'll see things happening that you wouldn't otherwise have noticed: for example, the first piece of mischief that Archimago arranges is to send the imitation Una into the bed of the Redcrosse Knight. She is "most like that virgin true" (I.i.49). She is an exact imitation of the true Church. This is central to the theme. The Roman Catholic Church, as represented later by Duessa, is really a bogus imitation of the true Catholic Church, which is, of course, what England has. So the Redcrosse Knight, having had Una at the beginning of the Book, has already lost her, quite early on, and has had this sham put in her place.

In canto ii we have the first description of Duessa (stanzas 12,13). Here she comes through, very clearly, as the Whore of Babylon, the Scarlet Woman of the Book of Revelations:

> A goodly Lady clad in scarlot red,
> Purfled with gold and pearle of rich assay,
> And like a *Persian* mitre on her hed
> She wore. . .
>
> ii. 13.

If you look at any of the medieval, English illuminated Apocalypses, of which there are some very beautiful examples, you will see pictures of Una and Duessa. Una is the Woman clothed with the sun and Duessa is the Scarlet Woman. It's rather curious to see, as it were, these illustrations of Book I of the *Faerie Queene* painted three centuries before Spenser was even born. You see the strength of this iconographical tradition surrounding the Book of Revelation. Here it is given the historical dimension that Duessa, the Scarlet Woman, is, quite simply, the Roman Church, and Una is the true Church, the Woman clothed with the sun who had to go into the wilderness and was later restored. That's the general theme, as Duessa more or less says herself — She was

> Borne the sole daughter of an Emperour,
> He that the wide West under his rule has,
> And high hath set his throne, where *Tiberis* doth pas.
>
> I.ii.22.

That, of course, is meant to be contrasted to Una's description of her parentage:

> . . . by descent from Royall lynage came
> Of ancient Kings and Queenes, that had of yore
> Their scepters stretcht from East to Westerne shore. . .
>
> I.i.5.

In other words, Una is universal, claiming East and West, whereas Duessa claims only the West. She represents the heretical Church of Rome.

If you look through the Book with this in mind — not only this, of course — you'll see, again and again, allusions to Church history. There is the story of Abessa, for example. She's not, as used to be said, a corrupt abbess but stands for absenteeism, "abesse," to be away. There's Kirkrapine, also; all the sacrilege, the misuse of Church funds, associated with the Roman Church up to the Reformation, all that comes in, quite naturally, as part of the anti-Romanist tendency of the Book. The rescue of Una from the satyrs is a little allegory of the way the Church fell for a time into the hands of people who knew only a "barbarous truth" (vi.12) — namely, I suppose, into the hands of people like the medieval heretics — the Waldensians, the Albigensians and so on. She is rescued by Satyrane, who is elaborately set up as a figure who is both natural and culti-vated, his father a savage man, his mother a cultivated lady. It is this blend of culture and nature which seems to be represented by the English Church.

More important, and with more apocalyptic details, and many references to the Book of Revelation, is the subjection, which I won't go into, of the Redcrosse Knight to Orgoglio. That is part of the Everyman aspect of the story, too. The Redcrosse Knight falls victim to his own pride. But the three months — and I think this is shown by the very large number of references in the text to the Book of Revelation — represents the three hundred years in which the English people were in captivity to the Popes, between Gregory VII in the eleventh century and Wyclif in the fourteenth.

The conclusion of the entire Book is clearly apocalyptic, with the slaying of the dragon, the harrowing of Hell and the apocalyptic marriage of Redcrosse to Una — all these were regularly allegorized in commentaries on the Book of Revelations as the restoration of the true Church of England, and all became part of the business of praising the Elizabethan Settlement, which was obviously very necessary, simply in order to try to restore political stability in the country. So you see, there is an immediate political end in all this use of the Book of Revelation. But I won't spend much time on Book I because I want to spend the rest of the time talking about Book V, with which I think you are probably less familiar.

The fifth Book is the Book of Justice and I don't think Spenser made quite such a good job of it as he did of the first three Books. He reverted, in this Book — if he wrote them all in the right order, which he almost certainly didn't — to the pattern that he uses in the first and second Books. He gives up the interlaced pattern of Books III and IV to a large extent. He takes what is for once a genuine Aristotelian virtue, namely Justice, and begins to expound it fairly systematically. He has a Knight of Justice — Artegall — and many examples of Justice in action. He has a core canto which is, as usual, the seventh, and which is a particularly difficult one. There's a great deal of political allegory of a rather immediate nature. For example, Duessa here represents Mary, Queen of Scots. Her trial in the Court of Chancery is clearly alluded to. So too is the Elizabethan intervention in the wars of the Netherlands. All these things come in quite transparent guise.

However, it would be unlike Spenser to write straightforward political allegory and he doesn't do that. You can see this from the way he starts Book V. He starts it with an unusually long proem about Justice and about the contrast between the present state of the world and its original state, long ago, in the Golden Age, and how much it has declined. This links up with the idea of mutability, too: how the

. . . heauens reuolution

Is wandred farre from where it first was pight. . .   st. 4.

It is pervaded by this rather general gloom that is characteristic of Spenser when he is thinking about how bad things have got. Curiously he can do all that and also imply that things have got very good since the accession of Elizabeth and the Elizabethan Settlement. This is characteristic of Spenser; the mood flows in these different ways.

You'll notice that the end of the poem is addressed directly to the Queen. We are first told that Justice is the most sacred of the Virtues:

Most sacred virtue she of all the rest,
Resembling God in his imperial might;

st. 10.

And then, in the final stanza, the address:

Dread Souerayne Goddesse, that doest highest sit
In seat of Judgement, in th'Almighties stead. . .

st. 11.

He adopts a very courtier-like tone. Having established the importance of the virtue of Justice and its relationship to Elizabeth, and her relationship to Astraea — which, incidentally, comes in immediately in the 11th stanza of the first canto with the story of how Astraea left the Earth because men had grown so wicked, and now hangs in the sky as the sign of the Virgin — he begins his myth of how Astraea trains the heroic agents of Justice, Artegall, Bacchus and Hercules. Hercules is a great shadowy figure behind this Book, as he is behind much Renaissance epic. He is the ideal hero; the hero who, as a young man and given the choice between vice and virtue, chose rightly the steep, upward path. This is not simply the Hercules that we know from ancient Greek literature. He acquired accretions of allegory in this period and became associated, for example, with Empire. It became built into the whole royal myth. Hercules is behind the whole of this Book, including his lapses. The entire story of Artegall's subjection to the power of Radigund and dressed as a woman and set to spin is based on the story of Hercules and Omphale.

None of this seems to me to be of very great importance. The theme takes a long time to develop seriously in this Book. The first canto gives you a quest — as it always does — the quest for Grantorto. This is exactly the figure you'd expect the Knight of Justice to strike down. Irena stands for the peace which will be the reward. There's an interesting invention in this part of the Book in the figure of Talus. He is a sort of mechanical man with a flail, who is the executive power of Justice. He has no feelings about what he is doing but simply goes and beats people up. He is entirely under the control of the magistrate and has no initiative of his own and is therefore represented as non-human and carrying this enormous weapon. I'll come back to Talus later.

What I want to emphasize is how simple the exemplary material is, as in, for example, the overthrow of Munera and Pollenta; examples of distributive justice on the one hand and of retributive justice on the other. These are the two major divisions of Justice in operation in the thought of the time. Distributive justice is when you adjudicate between parties who have rival claims on goods, for example, and retributive involves the punishment of wrongdoers. You can see a little vignette of that, incidentally, at the beginning of *King Lear*. Lear starts off as a figure of Justice, distributing his property, and then becomes retributive when he bans Cordelia and banishes Kent and so on.

The most interesting moment in this expository part of the Book is to do with the attack on communism, because that's what it really comes to, in the assault on the Giant who proclaims that he's going to level everything. This is in the second canto. This Giant really is a communist — an Anabaptism, probably — and he represents what the establishment were really very frightened of, extreme puritanical movements like the Family of Love and the Anabaptists, who thought that all property (and all women, for that matter) should be held in common. They held that that was the law of nature and vouched for by the law of God. Artegall comes up with a very sophisticated argument, saying you can't have equality without inequality, so to speak: you have to have hills as well as valleys. And then Talus simply goes in and destroys this Giant. This was a Giant of Democracy, or Communism. Democracy was a hated word in Elizabethan England — and later. It didn't seem conceivable to most people that something ruled by the mob could be anything but horrible. Order was conceived of as essentially hierarchical, and this is common to Hooker as well as Spenser, and indeed to most other people, including Milton, who although anti-monarchist was certainly not a democrat. He belived in an aristocracy within a republic. The difference between the views of Milton and Spenser is simply a difference as to the nature of monarchy.

The attack on democracy, levelling, interestingly prefigures a lot that was going to happen in England in the next half-century, when the Levellers became quite important among the factions involved with the Commonwealth. The idea that you can't have everything equal is, of course, a commonplace Elizabethan idea. You've got to have order and degree and all that is familiar from the Elizabethan World Picture.

It's after these examples, and after Artegall has fallen into the clutches of Radigund, and Britomart has set out to rescue him, that we come to the really crucial canto, namely the seventh. This canto has a certain sort of distinction, I think, in that of all the puzzles in the *Faerie Queene* it is the one that least lends itself to a solution. There have been a couple of books written about Book

V lately and it is interesting that both of them manage to avoid, somehow, what's meant to happen in the seventh canto. It's a difficult story. It's the story of Britomart coming to Isis Church. This Church, as it's called in the Argument, is a temple of Justice. And Spenser has in mind a famous allegory of Plutarch's, called *About Isis and Osiris,* which is very important for him and which he used also in the Garden of Adonis canto (sixth) in the third Book. Here the relationship between Isis and Osiris becomes the relationship between Equity and Justice.

I'm not an expert on legal history, but it is important to see what these two terms meant. It didn't simply mean you dealt justice and then applied clemency. Equity is not just being fair. It is a good deal more than that. In English law, Equity comes second, as it were, partly because of the enormous importance of the Common Law. But in all countries which are based on the tradition of Roman Law, Equity is regarded as the higher power, and indeed it is in Spenser. There's an old legal saying *summa jus, summa injuria,* the higher the law, the higher the injury, meaning that the law itself tends to create injustice. But the English maxim that equity follows the law is not generally accepted. The law is regarded as an instrument of equity. However, in England at the time when Spenser was writing, there was the Common Law on the one side and the Prerogative Courts, so-called, two of them, on the other: the Court of Chancery and the Court of Star Chamber. Now these two were not bound by precedent as, of course, the Common Law was, and they were also regarded as the Queen's Courts. It was said that the Court of Chancery was the voice of the Queen's conscience. The Star Chamber Court was used very often to stop people from doing things. It wasn't much used to make life easier, though of course this was one of the theoretical functions of these Courts. In a day when great men could easily bribe jurors and others it was very important to have a Court where this coudn't happen. So they did have some use. The Star Chamber was a very hated Court, however, and it was abolished as soon as possible, in 1642. It is represented in the fifth Book of the *Faerie Queene* by the poet who has his tongue nailed to a post in the Mercilla canto (ix.25). This was the sort of thing Elizabeth did. If someone said things she didn't like she might cut their ears off, for example, and this would be done through the Court of Star Chamber. It was an Equity Court, but, as you see, it wasn't always particularly beneficial to the people who appeared before it.

I mention this so that we can understand, and I don't claim to be able to explain in full, just what Spenser was talking about when he made Artegall the crocodile Justice, and Britomart the goddess Equity. Their sexual union, which Britomart sees in a vision, figures the intimate coming together of Justice and

Equity, which is presumably what Elizabeth has achieved since Britomart really turns into Queen Elizabeth in the course of the canto. The priests are rather puzzling. They're obviously the priests of Justice, but why they have long hair and all the rest of it is a subject of much dispute. There is puzzlement, too, over the connection between matter, which Britomart also represents, and Equity and the crocodile. All these things are much discussed and there is not really any final answer. All that I am emphasizing this for is to explain that there are points in the allegory of the *Faerie Queene*, which are still unsolved. There's even in the sixth stanza of canto vii an additional puzzlement. The last line reads:

That with her wreathed taile her middle did enfold.

To my mind it ought to be "*his* wreathed taile" but the reading has stuck and been defended by editors and it's still in the Oxford text. It seems to me to make the thing even harder unless you read "his wreathed taile."

The priests of the goddess Isis don't eat flesh and they don't drink wine. They don't drink wine because that is thought to spring from the "bloud of the Gyants" (st. 10). These are the Titans who were slain in their battle with the gods. The crocodile, too, is born of the earth by the action of the sun on the Nile mud, so both the crocodile and the wine represent something natural that's also bad. Wine would cause another rebellion, or so it's feared, and that's why the priests do without it; and the crocodile obviously stands for something bad as well as for the force of law. Incidentally, Talus has been left out of the temple for some reason, on which you might like to speculate. The giants, by the way, are very important in Book V. They represent rebelliousness, inequity and so on.

In the vision that Britomart has, she herself is converted, first into a priest and then into a goddess. The vision is puzzling, but when she tells the priest about it he sees through it immediately and recognizes her true identity and the progenitress of the English Queen:

Magnificke Virgin, that in queint disguise
Of British armes doest maske thy royall blood,
So to persue a perillous emprize;

V.vii. 21.

The Priest then explains the dream to her. He says:

For that same Crocodile doth represent
Thy righteous Knight, that is thy faithfull louer,
Like to *Osyris* in all iust endeuer.
For that same Crocodile *Osyris* is,
That under *Isis* feete doth sleep for euer:

22.

It's quite clear, however, that the priest's explanation of the dream is not adequate because there are so many things he leaves out, for example the great storm and the curious behaviour of the crocodile. He's not "under Isis feete" sleeping for ever. Far from it; he does quite a number of things in the course of the dream. So, you see, Spenser is here offering only a partial explanation and the true meaning may rest in some sort of contemporary row that was going on about law. There was a row going on among the Common lawyers who all thought that the Prerogative Courts were getting uppish and were taking power away from them. The Prerogative Courts were also associated with this growing idea of Imperial power of the Queen. This all became very much more serious in the next reign, that of James I. It all related to the notion that the King was above the law, which was put into action rather disastrously when Charles I decided to close down Parliament and so on. All this is central to English history. It was an important argument for Spenser because as an Imperialist, which in a sense he was, he would clearly be attracted by the notion of Prerogative Courts. He himself, incidentally, was an officer of the Court of Chancery in Ireland.

Here again we are back with an immediate political issue, a controversial Elizabethan issue, all dressed up, as was the custom, in myth and allegory and yet, for all that dream-like, visionary quality, not lacking in relevance to the historical events of the time.

The same is true of the very fine canto that deals with Mercilla who is dealing justice to Mary, Queen of Scots. Mary, Queen of Scots was tried in a prerogative court (the Court of Chancery), not under Common Law, and here Mercilla is presented very splendidly as bearing all the Regalia associated with the Crown — the rusty sword, the sceptre (ix.30) — and given this huge "Maestà" quality; she is enthroned in splendour with Duessa before her. Then you are immediately led into contemporary history when Mercilla can't make up her mind at the end to condemn Duessa, who is now simply Mary, Queen of Scots. And then everybody goes off to the Netherlands and fights the Spanish. So the Book ends as a rather thin, transparent, political allegory. Of course, Grantorto is finally slain. I don't think the Book can compare in depth or interest with the first, but that is partly because the first used everything up in a rather prodigal way. The greatest interest of this Book is, I think, in the seventh canto and in the Mercilla passages and they are worth a good deal of your attention and interpretation.

II

THE FAERIE QUEENE

STEPHEN FENDER

I've forgotten the precise name of this lecture, but it is about history and authentication. The reason why I've chosen to give it, and to think about it, is because I want to grapple with the curious role that it seems to me history plays in the *Faerie Queene*.

I'll define my terms: they're very simple, not at all recherché. They're simply the words "fact," "history" and "romance." By "facts" I mean something that happens in fiction which appears to the reader to have a verifiable existence outside fiction. So that the Battle of Borodino in *War and Peace* may be called a fact, even though we do not know who won it or any details. We think we know it happened, and that's what I mean by "fact." "History" is simply a fact that happened in the past, or a string of facts, which are verifiable. Again I am talking about these phenomena as they occur in fiction. Finally, I am using "romance" in its literary sense, as in the Oxford English Dictionary, "a fictitious narrative in which the scenes and incidents are very remote from those of ordinary life." This definition is useful because it includes Shakespeare's late plays, two of which I shall be mentioning briefly. So you see what I am interested in: scenes in romance, narratives remote from everyday existence, which nevertheless we can take as verifiable incidents.

Now, my thesis is very simple and it is that in some romances facts and history, when they occur, authenticate the romance. They make it more realistic and convincing. And in other cases the appearance of facts or history in romance makes it less realistic, more obviously a fiction. They set it off or frame it, or as Brecht would say, they "alienate" the romance.

I'll give you a couple of examples. The first is from *The Last of the Mohicans*, by Fenimore Cooper, which is an early American romance. The first extract is from the text:

Haward took the gourd, and after swallowing a little of the water, threw it aside with grimaces of discontent. The Scout laughed at his silent, but heartfelt, manner and shook his head with vast satisfaction.

"Ah, you want the flavour that one gets by habit; time was when I liked it as little as yourself; but I have come to my taste, and I now crave it, as a deer does the licks. Your high spiced wines are not better liked than a redskin relishes this water; especially when his natur' is ailing. But Uncas has made his fire and it is time we think of eating, for our journey is long, and all before us."

Interrupting the dialogue by this abrupt transition, the scout had instant recourse to the fragments of food that had escaped the voracity of the Hurons. A very summary process completed the simple cookery, when he and the Mohicans commenced their humble meal, with the silence and characteristic diligence of men who ate in order to enable themselves to endure great and unremitting toil.

When this necessary, and, happily, grateful duty had been performed, each of the foresters stooped and took a long and parting draught of that solitary and silent spring, around which, and its sister fountains, within fifty years, the wealth, beauty and talents of a hemisphere were able to assemble in throngs, in pursuit of health and pleasure. Then Hawkeye announced his determination to proceed.

There are several interesting things here beside the point for our purposes today. There's the very interesting disjunction of styles. The narrator chooses to take an extremely high-falutin' and East Coast style, whereas he allows his characters (as did Mark Twain later) to speak various dialects. But the main point is that at the bottom of the page are two notes. These are not notes provided by a later editor; they are notes provided by the author and are in fact part of the text and were in the first edition. The first note glosses "lick":

Many of the animals of the American forests resort to those spots where salt springs are found. These are called "licks" or "salt licks," in the language of the country, from the circumstance that the quadruped is often obliged to lick the earth in order to obtain the saline particles. These licks are great places of resort with the hunters, who waylay their game near the paths that lead to them.

Footnote 2 glosses the springs that he refers to:

> The scene of the foregoing incidents is on the spot where the village of Ballston now stands; one of the two principal watering-places in America.

What was the effect of this for a reader in the 1840's or '50's? I think, among other things, he would get a clear sense of his own country's legendary past, maybe referring to only one hundred to one hundred and fifty years earlier, and a modern, civilizing, urban presence which is already beginning to obliterate that past. What the footnote does there, in bringing history or actuality into the story — rather crudely, but it is definitely brought in — is to frame the story, to frame the time in which it takes place, and its events, making it seem more special and more remote. It's an interesting effect and it's repeated again and again through *The Last of the Mohicans,* which has to do with a story which took place about one hundred years before the author's own youth. Long enough ago to seem, in the fast moving historical imagination of the Americans in the early nineteenth century, legendary.

So prevalent was this habit of inserting actuality in the romance that the dime novels did it as well, much more comically. For instance, *Seth Jones* by Edward S. Ellis. This is obviously sub-Cooper, there's no question about that. This extract is taken from the main body of the text:

> We mention in this place that the Indians who had captured Ina were, as Seth had remarked, members of the Mohawk tribe. This tribe itself was a member of the "Five Nations," including with them the Seneca, the Cayuga, Onondaga and Oneida tribes, which had become quite famous in history. They are known among the French as the *Iroquois,* among the Dutch as the *Maguas,* while at home they are called Mingoes, or Agamuschim, signifying *The United People.*

Etcetera, etcetera. Then Chapter Five begins and we are back with the story. Seth Jones and Graham exchange some dialogue:

> "The Mohawks, you say, have then captured her?" remarked Graham after a moment's pause.
> "Yes! I know it's them!"
> "Did you get a glimpse of them?"
> "I came up as soon as possible, and they were leaving at that moment. I saw one or two of them and know'd it was them, sure 'nough. Howsumever, that don't make no difference, whether it's the Mohawks or the Oneidas or any of them blasted Five Nation niggers. They're all a set of skunks, and one would as lief run off with a man's gal as not. There ain't no difference atwixt 'em."

Well, the author thinks there's a difference atwixt 'em, but the hero doesn't.

Here there's an extreme disjunction, clearly, between what matters in the verifiable world of anthropology and what happens in the world of fiction. But it was thought necessary, curiously so perhaps, to provide a scholarly footnote. Incidentally, these are the Indians that Cooper's writing about as well, so if you don't use the scholarly footnote for Seth Jones it comes in handy for *The Last of the Mohicans*. They are always going on about the Five Nations, or the Mingoes in a very confusing way in the Leatherstocking romances.

This is curious, obviously. There's an extreme dislocation here. I am simply trying to take an extreme case, but you see the difference between this and the kind of narrative which roots you in some kind of realism and then lets you see the wider implications behind or through realism. We are not dealing with that at all. This is not a case where you get totally caught up in, for instance, the history of Napoleon's invasion of Russia in *War and Peace*, and begin to see general truths, or just romantic fictions, behind or through the history. The American books from which I read, and especially the latter, present a case where the facts and the romance are totally separate, explicitly separate, yet both there.

Why, I wonder? I am not picking out two rather odd American examples. This sort of thing happens again and again. Think for instance of the James Bond stories which are extremely unrealistic; they are impossible. And yet they are very accurate as to some particular details — kinds of guns, kinds of cars; they are very accurate about the particular calibre of semi-automatic pistol that so-and-so uses, and somebody else is issued with a Smith and Wesson .357 Magnum using dum-dum bullets. All this might be taken out of *Guns and Ammo,* or some such place. Likewise cars: it doesn't mention mythical cars. It may be an Aston Martin wondrously modified, but it's nevertheless an Aston Martin, a real make. Yet all the rest is thoroughly unrealistic. Why?

You could say, I suppose, that it's an attempt to ballast the romance in some way — though that doesn't seem to me to get us very far. I think, myself, that in the case of the *Mohicans,* the facts do really alienate the fiction in the way that Brecht meant. That is, it sets it aside, and reminds you that what you are reading, what you are getting wrapped up in, is really very different from actual life; it is separate. It seems to me it works like those curious lines or half-lines, or sometimes five or six lines, that you get at the end of Shakespeare's comedies. Thus at the end of *Twelfth Night,* for instance, after everyone has been married and gone off in new harmony and concord, you get Feste coming in and singing a wry little song whose refrain is "The rain it raineth every day." It is a kind of shifting of gears down to real life again, getting the audience accustomed to the ordinary workaday world where there is winter as well as summer, and bad weather as well as good.

But you have to account for this again. It isn't there simply for ballast. It seems that it does have something in common with the footnotes in *The Last of the Mohicans,* and the *Seth Jones* example as well. It frames the fiction and alienates the audience. It makes you realize that what you've seen, in the case of *Twelfth Night,* is very special and very fragile, unrealistic, a fiction. It doesn't mean that it makes you dislike it, or that it changes the tone towards the characters or any of these things. We're not using the usual terminology of literary criticism at all here. We're talking about the kind of emotional feeling that you get at the end; not about the characters but about the whole structure. That, again, is quite different from, for instance, medieval allegory — like Henryson's *Two Mice* or the marriage debate in the *Canterbury Tales,* — where you can be totally engaged in the realistic (I don't mean factual) surface story, at the same time realizing that it has other meanings. The marriage debate in the *Canterbury Tales* is also about the nature of marriage, not just about the Wife of Bath's quirks. It's also about the nature of Christ and his Church — this is a possible interpretation which works out consistently. It has, in other words, an allegorical but also an analogical and even tropological level. All medieval allegory is meant to have four levels as the *Canterbury Tales* does, and Henryson's *Moral Fables,* but at no point is the tissue of realism lifted from the wider issues. What we're dealing with in both the cases I shall be talking about — that is where the facts authenticate or the facts alienate — is a situation where the factual material is quite separate and is set out as separate from the narrative.

I've given you two examples where I think the fiction is alienated by the factual material. I want to give you one that works in a different way now. Imagine yourself in 1613, going along to the Globe Theatre and, assuming that the Globe Theatre didn't actually burn down during a production of this play — which it did — let's assume you sit through to the end of *Henry VIII.* Queen Elizabeth had died in 1603; that's as long ago for the play's first audience as the Kennedy period is for us now. In *Henry VIII* the birth of Elizabeth occurs. Assuming, then, that the theatre had survived the marvellous cannon fight and got through to Act V, how do you think you would react to this? Cranmer comes in bearing the new-born Elizabeth in his arms and addresses the King:

Let me speak, sir.
For heaven now bids me; and the words I utter
Let none think flattery, for they'll find 'em truth.
This royal infant — heaven still move about her! —
Though in her cradle, yet now promises
Upon this land a thousand thousand blessings,
Which time shall bring to ripeness. She shall be —

But few now living can behold that goodness —
A pattern to all princes living with her,
And all that shall succeed. . .

She shall be lov'd and fear'd. Her own shall bless her:
Her foes shake like a field of beaten corn,
And hang their heads with sorrow. Good grows with her;
In her days every man shall eat with safety
Under his own vine what he plants, and sing
The merry song of peace to all his neighbours. . .

King   Thou speakest wonders.
Cran.   She shall be, to the happiness of England,
An aged princess; many days shall see her,
And yet no day without a deed to crown it.
Would I had known no more! But she must die —
She must, the saints must have her — yet a virgin;
A most unspotted lily shall she pass
To the'ground, and all the world shall mourn her.

V.iv. 14-62

Well, how's it working? Shakespeare's using a very clever device here. This is not, I admit, a romance, though it's one of the late plays and it's a way of getting into something which does happen more often in the romance. Shakespeare's always looking for ways of authenticating the most wondrous miraculous things he puts in his last plays. I shall come to another example at the end.

How do you react to the extract above? I think (and this is obviously, and for many reasons, just guess-work) that there would be very few people watching that play who wouldn't have been alive for at least part of Elizabeth's reign. You'd have had to have been under ten to have missed spending at least part of your life in Elizabeth's reign. So everybody over ten years old hearing this speech would feel that he could verify it. I don't mean that he could *in fact* verify it, but that he would feel that he could. Probably when he lived in Elizabeth's reign he didn't feel that everything was marvellous. He didn't feel that her foes were shaking like "a field of beaten corn," or that he was eating "in safety under his own vine." It was a time of great turmoil and great insecurity and he probably didn't think at the time, any more than we do now, that he was living in a time of great peace and security.

Yet we all know there's a human tendency to look back ten, fifteen, twenty years ago to a better age, or at least a better time than we now live in. When an old lady says she's sure there was a time when the post was delivered on time, and when we had long, hot summers, and snowy Christmases, she is partly right and partly wrong. She may be right about the post, to be sure, but she's building it into a much happier system — she's writing a novel of her own life. The point I'm making is that there's a difference between things we think we can verify and things which we think are just stories to which we may or may not acquiesce. If someone gets up, ten years after the death of Queen Elizabeth and utters a prophecy which is much more wonderful and exaggerated than could be credited as possible, and we can apparently — though not really — verify this retrospectively, this is a device of authentication rather than alienation. You bring history, or what passes for verifiable facts, into a very optimistic, and indeed romantic, prophecy — certainly an improbable prophecy — and the effect is to authenticate it. Notice that the King says, "Thou speakest wonders," and Cranmer goes on with his prophecy as though he was recounting mere facts. We are aware both of the King's amazement and what appears to be the literal truth of the amazing things that Cranmer is saying. We must watch for this device again and again in Shakespeare's later plays.

This is also, I think, what is happening in *The Faerie Queene*, and I'm now going to take two examples of the same thing: history or facts being brought in to authenticate, not to alienate, the fiction. The first case I want to take is in Book I. Now you all know, and you have all read, that *The Faerie Queene* is a particular, and a general, allegory. It has two kinds of allegory. Spenser says in the Letter to Raleigh, "In that Faerie Queene I meane glory in my general intention, but in my particular I conceiue the most excellent and glorious person of our soueraine the Queene." So the Faerie Queene stands for a general abstract quality and for a particular person. Likewise, Duessa stands for falsehood, as we're told, but also for Mary, Queen of Scots (in Book V) and in some intermediate denotation for the Roman Catholic Church. The Redcrosse Knight stands for Holiness and also St. George. Now, who is St. George? He's a kind of historical figure, legendary perhaps, but certainly taken as a real figure in English history by Spenser's contemporary readers. So he, too, has both an historical role and an unhistorical abstract meaning, holiness.

In a medieval romance you might expect that the Redcrosse Knight should be realized — identified — as St. George from the beginning. It would be called *The Pilgrimage of St. George* or *The Adventures of St. George,* with lots of other narratives interlaced, to be sure, but with St. George, the reader would be shown other qualities, like holiness, or battling with evil, when St. George fights the dragon, and so on. But that's not what Spenser does at all. It's true he calls the Redcrosse Knight St. George, from time to time earlier on, but in fact he starts us off in an extremely placeless, timeless, even, some would maintain, plotless story.

Spenser's opening line, "A Gentle Knight was pricking on the plaine," is meant to be an epic beginning, *in medias res*, but there's more to it than that, because if you look at the beginning of the *Odyssey,* "A gentle sailor was rolling on the main" or whatever, you very quickly get a clear sense of where he's going, where he's been, what his mates look like and the actual physical adventures they are having. This is not the case with *The Faerie Queene* at all. Where are they going? They're going to release Una's parents who are trapped by some sort of fiend. But, as we all know, this soon dissolves into nothing. He has adventures, but they "pop up," like figures in shooting galleries, and then pop down again. It's almost like *Waiting for Godot.* Rather than going somewhere over a plain, they might as well be standing still and having various events pass them by. As far as a sense of time is concerned, I don't get any. I don't even get a sense of day and night except, in their obvious symbolic representation, night-time and darkness is the time you're likely to go astray, and daytime is the time you can see things as they really are.

This is one of the reasons, I think, why people are disappointed by the poem. They are told by the *faux naif* school to read it for the story, and they find there isn't any story — at least in the first six or eight cantos of Book I — and there isn't a place, and there isn't what you can call a sequence of events. There is a considerable difference between the kind of complexity that you get in the *Orlando Furioso,* with lots and lots of stories rolled together, and the kind of complexity which you get in *The Faerie Queene.*

Not until cantos viii and ix, when Arthur first appears and tells his history (ix), do you get a real narrative, or a narrative more like a romance story. It's not very long, simply Arthur's life and how he comes to be chasing or hunting for the Faerie Queene. It includes that marvellous episode of his dream when the Faerie Queene came to him in a vision. It also mentions, for the first time, real places, places of which we have heard; the River Dee, in Cheshire and North Wales, is mentioned. This is, as far as I know, the first place-name that is actually verifiable in the story. After that, also, it is interesting to note — though it may not be significant — that the characters are introduced in a rather different way. It is after Arthur's story that the Redcrosse Knight encounters Despair. He encounters him via Sir Trevisan, and Sir Trevisan is introduced cinematographically, realistically, from the point of view of one of the characters. First you see a man riding, then you see he hasn't got a helmet, then you see his hair streaming out behind and, finally, as he gets up to you you see that he is afraid and that he has a story to tell. This is quite unlike the way the earlier characters "pop up." Granted this is not maintained, but you're getting a mixture, a density of different kinds of narrative mode that you didn't have in the earlier part of the story.

Most important of all, however, is what happens in the House of Holiness and the Vision of the New Jerusalem, because here's a case where I can say with absolute confidence that there's no question but that the author here is violating our expectations. The old man has taken Redcrosse up to the highest mount, after they've been through the House of Holiness and all its purging effects, and shows him the vision of the New Jerusalem:

That done, he leads him to the highest Mount;
Such one, as that same mighty man of God,
That bloud-red billowes like a walled front
On either side disparted with his rod,
Till that his army dry-foot through them yod,
Dwelt fortie dayes vpon; wher writ in stone
With bloudy letters by the hand of God,
The bitter doome of death and balefull mone
He did receiue, whiles flashing fire about him shone.

I.x.53.

There then follows a stanza of epic comparisons. Then he sees the city:

Faire knight (quoth he) *Hierusalem* that is,
The new *Hierusalem,* that God has built
For those to dwell in, that are chosen his,
His chosen people purg'd from sinfull guilt,
With pretious bloud, which cruelly was spilt
On cursed tree, of that vnspotted lam,
That for the sinnes of all the world was kilt:
Now are they Saints all in that City sam,
More deare vnto their God, then younglings to their dam.

57

Till now, said then the knight, I weened well,
That great *Cleopolis,* where I haue beene,
In which that fairest *Faeire Queene* doth dwell,
The fairest Citie was, that might be seene;
And that bright towre all built of christall cleene,
Panthea, seemed the brightest thing, that was:
But now by proofe all otherwise I weene;
For this great Citie that does far surpas,

And this bright Angels towre quite dims that towre of glas.

58

Cleopolis is, of course, London. This is the point at which, to use a slightly
trendy, but in this case accurate, term, Spenser interrupts the syntax of his
narrative. How should this narrative sentence be completed? Cast your memories
back now to the story. The Redcrosse Knight is being perfected, isn't he? His
pilgrimage is one of self-perfection. It has been something like a morality play, a
bit like *Everyman* where the characters are abstractions, and they are all to do
with the eschatology, the science of last things; it's all about his salvation. So, of
course, once he has reached the House of Holiness, he has only to die and go to
the New Jerusalem. This is a vision of where he should be going next. So the
obvious end of this "sentence" is that he should die, pass over the river, or
whatever, and go to the New Jerusalem. But that's not what happens, and the
interruption is made explicit, because the old man pulls him back and says:

Most trew, then said the holy aged man;
Yet is *Cleopolis,* for earthly frame,
The fairest peece, that eye beholden can:
And well beseems all knights of noble name,
That couet in th'immortall booke of fame
To be eternized, that same to haunt,
And doen their seruice to that soueraigne Dame,
That glorie does to them for guerdon graunt:
For she is heauenly borne, and heuen may iustly vaunt.

I.x. 59

And thou faire ymp, sprong out from English race,
How euer now accompted Elfins sonne,
Well worthy doest thy seruice for her grace,
To aide a virgin desolate foredonne.
But when thou famous victorie hast wonne,
And high emongst all knights hast hong thy shield,
Thenceforth the suit of earthly conquest shonne,
And wash thy hands from guilt of bloudy field:
For bloud can nought but sin, and wars but sorrowes yield.

60

Then seeke this path, that I to thee presage,
Which after all to heauen shall thee send. . .

And then he goes on to say it is time for you to take your place in history; to
become St. George, to advance the fortunes of the English race. (Redcrosse is
here identified as English for the first time.) Again the readers could feel they

verify it. "So *that's* how it was." "*That's* who he was." "*That's* how it happened." The rest is known through legends. This is certainly semi-historical, isn't it? It is quite different from the placeless, timeless events that have occurred up till now. Now he's got a name, a role in history, a place in time. I'm not saying we stick with this barely historical level to the end of Book I, but now that it has been mixed in we can't get rid of it. Now everything that's happening to the Redcrosse Knight is also happening to St. George, who, of course, we know. Everything that's happening to the Redcrosse Knight is now history, because it belongs to a historical/legendary character.

You see how this happens? It's quite similar to the *Henry VIII* effect, because it relates directly to what the audience or reader feel they can verify about their own history, their own lives.

Now I'm going to take another case which is more elaborate and more important, I think. It's over a much larger narrative span and really shows that Spenser is consciously using the effect. It comes from Book III and describes the curious business of what happens to Britomart when she sees the image of her lover in a mirror. The sequence of events is most important here and their parallel with similar events in the *Orlando Furioso.* I'll take the latter first. In canto iii of *Orlando Furioso,* Bradamante, who is obviously a main source for Britomart, visits the strange tomb built by Merlin. A voice speaks out of the tomb and predicts that she will bear a lineage that, in Harington's translation:

shall restore

By warlike feats the glory shining bright

That Italy possessed heretofore;

That's quite different, of course, from the historical projection in *The Faerie Queene,* because when the Italian reader read that, he did not know that Italian glory would be restored, and indeed it never was in the sense that Ariosto meant. So that was really a hope for a good future, not something that one could verify. That's the first difference. Secondly, the sequence in the *Orlando Furioso* is quite straightforward, while in *The Faerie Queene* this episode is sandwiched in among others which do not directly precede or follow it in the sequence of the story's events.

Just to remind you, I'll go over the first four cantos of Book III because I want you to meditate for a moment on the sequence of events. Britomart sets off and visits the Castle of Malecasta, or Castle Joyeous. She sees six liegemen of Malecasta, Guardante, Parlante, Basciante, etc., who represent the six stages of courtly love — looking, speaking, kissing, etc. So clearly the Castle of Malecasta is a bad place; it can be said to be opposed to chastity — not virginity, of course, but chastity. As you know, they go to dinner, and Malecasta, who thinks that

Britomart is a gentleman and not a lady, starts playing "footsie" with her under the table and later on at night slips off to her room and sneaks into bed with Britomart because she is overcome with passion. Britomart, of course, immediately throws her out, at which Malecasta sets up a great howl and her six liegemen come into the room and one of them wounds Britomart. The one who wounds her is Guardante — seeing. You all know about the sin of the eye; this is how Troilus falls for Criseyde, and this is what happens in *Midsummer Night's Dream*. There's a good deal of ambivalence about the power of sight.

Britomart then continues on with the Redcrosse Knight and tells why she is dressed up as a man and wandering so far from home, which is, of course, Britain. She says it's to do mighty deeds, and to search for Artegall who, she says, has done her dishonour, but whom, the reader is then told, she in fact saw in a magic mirror as an image of her future husband. Notice that the sequence is inverted to place the chronologically earlier mirror episode after the events in the Castle of Malecasta. Here you have something unusual happening which is then explained later. The second point is that we're also getting a preparation for the curious business of seeing Artegall in the mirror. The fact that she's wounded by Guardante is one fictional mode of saying that she is susceptible to the love of the eye.

Now we must look in more detail at what Britomart sees, and what people say about what she sees and says. First, let us look at the description of the mirror. This is a very odd stanza:

> It vertue had, to shew in perfect sight,
> What euer thing was in the world contaynd,
> Betwixt the lowest earth and heauens hight,
> So that it to the looker appertaynd;
> What euer foe had wrought, or friend had faynd,
> Therein discouered was, ne ought mote pas,
> Ne ought in secret from the same remaynd;
> For thy it round and hollow shaped was,
> Like to the world it selfe, and seem'd a world of glas.

III.ii.19.

(We'll have to leave that curious middle line.) Like the pool in the *Romance of the Rose,* this mirror shows everything in the garden or, in this case, in the world. It doesn't show just good things or just bad things, it shows everything with which the looker can fall in love. In the *Romance* there is an inscription around the pond which says that here it was that Narcissus fell in love with his own face and died. The lover looks in and sees at the bottom of the pool the whole of the garden reflected, half of it in one crystal hemisphere and half of it in the other. The lover chooses just one thing. Part of the meaning of the metaphor is that you have the whole world to choose from and you actually choose what aspect of it to fall in love with. Whether the choice is sensible or not is up to you. Depending on how you look, you might catch the light in a certain way and catch the reflection of your own face, or you might see through to the crystal to see the image of a rose, as the lover does. Whatever you do see, you will then magically, and inextricably, fall in love with it.

This is the first point to note. It is very close to the description of the pond in the *Romance of the Rose,* even to the negative example of Narcissus at the end. This is what Britomart sees:

> The Damzell well did vew his personage,
> And liked well, ne further fastned not,
> But went her way; ne her vnguilty age
> Did weene, vnwares, that her vnlucky lot
> Lay hidden in the bottome of the pot;
> Of hurt vnwist most daunger doth redound:
> But the false Archer, which that arrow shot
> So slyly, that she did not feele the wounde,
> Did smyle full smoothly at her weetlesse wofull stound.

III.ii 26

> Thenceforth the feather in her loftie crest,
> Ruffed of loue, gan lowly to auaile,
> And her proud portance, and her princely gest,
> With which she earst tryumphed, now did quaile:
> Sad, solemne, sowre, and full of fancies fraile
> She woxe; yet wist she neither how, nor why...

27

One of Britomart's explicit fears is explained in stanza 38.

> Nor man it is, nor other liuing wight;
> For then some hope I might vnto me draw,
> But th'only shade and semblant of a knight,
> Whose shape or person yet I neuer saw,
> Hath me subiected to loues cruell law:
> The same one day, as me misfortune led,
> I in my fathers wondrous mirrhour saw,
> And pleased with that seemingly goodly-hed,
> Vnwares the hidden hooke with baite I swallowed.

38

Britomart knows what she sees is not there and that worries her because it throws open two possibilities: she is seeing either a *phantasm* or an *oneiros,* to use the terms in Macrobius's *Commentary on the Dream of Scipio.* An *oneiros* is a vision of something truer than the fallen world. We can't see anything perfect around us because the world is fallen, but our conceptualizing intelligence can make out something very beautiful. These are illuminations, dreams of things that are even truer than our life around us. On the other hand it may simply be a *phantasm,* a gross delusion, a devilish mistake based on the wrong analysis of sense data.

Notice what the nurse says. Conventionally (compare the nurse in *Romeo and Juliet*), she tries to cheer up the girl a bit and has a sort of optimistic, neo-platonic solution to the problem:

Daughter (said she) what need ye be dismayd,
Or why make ye such monster of your mind?
Of much more vncouth thing I was affrayd;
Of filthy lust, contrarie vnto kind:
But this affection nothing straunge I find;
For who with reason can you aye reproue,
To loue the semblant pleasing most your mind,
And yield your heart, whence ye cannot remoue?
No guilt in you, but in the tyranny of loue.

40

What the nurse is saying is that she doesn't know whether it's a *phantasm* or an *oneiros,* but it's nice anyway. It's much better than if Britomart had imagined a terrible monster. At least it shows the projections of Britomart's mind are superior — he's a handsome man, speaks well, is well connected — it shows Britomart has the "right" kind of imagination. That might be, in an average book, the end of the affair, but it's not in this case. We have a kind of answer to whether the vision is good or bad, but Spenser is not satisfied. He wants not only to make it good, but to authenticate it.

He has Britomart go off to Merlin, who made the mirror, and knows how it works, to ask him what it was she saw. He says:

It was not, *Britomart,* thy wandring eye,
Glauncing vnwares in charmed looking glas,
But the streight course of heauenly destiny,
Led with eternall prouidence, that has
Guided thy glaunce, to bring his will to pas:
Ne is thy fate, ne is thy fortune ill,
To loue the prowest knight, that euer was.
Therefore submit thy wayes vnto his will,

And do by all dew meanes thy destiny fulfill.

III.iii.24.

How does he prove this to us? How does he demonstrate it? By history once
again:

The man whom heauens haue ordaynd to bee
The spouse of *Britomart,* is *Arthegall.*
He wonneth in the land of *Fayeree,*
Yet is no *Fary* borne, ne sib at all
To Elfes, but sprong of seed terrestriall,
And whilome by false *Faries* stolne away,
Whiles yet in infant cradel he did crall;
Ne other to himselfe is knowne this day,
But that he by an Elfe was gotten of a *Fay*.

26

Then he goes on with the prophecy. Britain — that is the Celtic, Brythonic part
of Britain deriving from Wales — will overcome the Saxon after twice four
hundred years. From Artegall to Cadwaller the Britons will hold sway, and then
will come the terrible period of Saxon rule, until:

There shall a sparke of fire, which hath long-while
Bene in his ashes raked vp, and hid,
Be freshly kindled in the fruitful Ile
Of *Mona,* where it lurked in exile;
Which shall a sparke of fire, which hath long-while
And reach into the house, that beares the stile
Of royall maiesty and soueraigne name;
So shall the Briton bloud their crowne againe reclaime.

48

Thenceforth eternall vnion shall be made
Betweene the nations different afore,
And sacred Peace shall louingly perswade
The warlike minds, to learne her goodly lore. . .

This is the theme of Hall's history, of course; it is the coming of the Tudors with
Henry VII. Spenser is extending the historical union of the Houses of Lancaster
and York into a grand reunion of Saxon and British. From then on will be the
millennium; there will be a time of peace and plenty.

Once again, the Elizabethan reader probably felt he could verify this. Perhaps
their daily lives did not bear evidence to such a time, but, looking back on the
whole period in the spirit evident in Shakespeare's history plays, the Tudor
period did represent a time of lasting peace and prosperity after the devastating

Wars of the Roses. I don't know, but there is an appeal, not, as in the *Orlando Furioso*, to a pious hope for the future of Italy, but to something that actually seemed to have happened and which could be passed off as verifiable. And therefore what Britomart sees in the wonderful mirror doesn't just stop with an analysis of its value (is it good or bad?), but it is actually authenticated by history. This is a stage further than what you might expect. It is similar, I think, to what you might get in Shakespeare's late plays and I'm just going to end with a reminder of what happens at the end of *The Winter's Tale*.

The end of *The Winter's Tale* is the marvellous unveiling of the statue of Hermione. The King is being reunited with his wife whom he insulted many years ago and who he thought was dead. It's important to note here just what changes Shakespeare is making. First of all he is changing his source, Greene's *Pandosto*, where the climax of the action is the discovery of a lost daughter. There is a lost daughter here, called Perdita, and she's also discovered, but that's not all of the action. There's the wife as well, made into a statue. The other innovation that Shakespeare makes is that he keeps a very important piece of exposition away from the audience. He doesn't tell the audience that Hermione, the wife, is still alive. When the statue's unveiled, we understand pretty quickly what's going on, but he doesn't *tell* us that she's alive. The effect seems to me to be marvellous. Hermione is unveiled, and Leontes, the King, says:

Her natural posture!
Chide me, dear stone, that I may say indeed
Thou art Hermione; or rather, thou art she
In thy not chiding; for she was as tender
As infancy and grace. But yet, Paulina,
Hermione was not so much wrinkled, nothing
So aged as this seems.
Polixenes: O, not by much!
Paulina: So much the more our carver's excellence,
Which lets go by some sixteen years and makes her
As she lived now.
Leontes: As now she might have done,
So much to my good confort, as it is
Now piercing to my soul. O, thus she stood,
Even with such life of majesty — warm life,
As now it coldly stands — when first I woo'd her!
I am asham'd. Does not the stone rebuke me
For being more stone that it? O royal piece,
There's magic in thy majesty, which has

My evils conjur'd to remembrance, and
From thy admiring daughter took the spirits,
Standing like stone with thee!
Perdita: And give me leave,
And do not say 'tis superstition that
I kneel, and then implore her blessing. Lady,
Dear Queen, that ended when I but began,
Give me that hand of yours to kiss.
Paulina: O, patience!
The statue is but newly fix'd, the colour's
Not dry.

V.3. 23-44.

They go on like this with the audience genuinely unsure, I suppose, but beginning to catch on. Leontes tells Paulina not to draw the curtain again, but Paulina
says:

No longer shall you gaze on't, lest your fancy
May think anon it moves.
Leontes: Let be, let be.
Would I were dead, but that methinks already —
What was he that did make it? See, my lord,
Would you not deem it breath'd, and that those veins
Did verily bear blood?
Polixenes: Masterly done!
The very life seems warm upon her lip.
Leontes: The fixture of her eye has motion in't,
As we are mock'd with art.

V.3. 60-68.

Now, at last, Paulina says:

Music awake her: strike.
'Tis time; descend; be stone no more; approach;
Strike all that look upon with marvel. Come;
I'll fill your grave up. Stir; nay, come away.

V.3. 98-101.

Hermione steps down from the plinth and Leontes says:
                    O, she's warm!
If this be magic, let it be an art
Lawful as eating.

Paulina replies:

> That she is living,
> Were it but told you, should be hooted at
> Like an old tale; but it appears she lives,
> Though yet she speak not. Mark a little while.
> Please you to interpose, fair madam. Kneel,
> And pray your mother's blessing. Turn, good lady;
> Our Perdita is found.

V.3. 109-121.

This seems to be a stage beyond the sort of happy solution you get in a Shakespeare comedy where, although it would be marvellous if it could happen, we know it can't. All are joined in harmony and all seems happy, and then comes "the rain it raineth every day" and we realize it's all fiction and we are now going out into life. This is quite different. Shakespeare has found a way of verifying the most impossible romance by revealing that Hermione is alive. It can be accounted for in three ways: either it's a wonder, or it's logical, or it's both a wonder *and* logical (perhaps there are wonders in logic; perhaps there are wonders in history). And that, it seems to me, is the effect. Shakespeare is moving beyond the methods of the comedies.

I think this is also what Spenser is doing. He is attempting to use history to authenticate a fiction, and this is quite different from the other examples we looked at, the final song in *Twelfth Night* or a James Bond story or *The Last of the Mohicans,* where the facts certainly have a place — they are not merely a sort of nervous gesture to reality — but are there because they set the fiction off.

III

DONNE: LECTURE ONE

FRANK KERMODE

I'm going to speak this morning fairly generally, but also ask you to look at two or three poems more carefully.

You remember that Professor Gombrich spoke at the beginning of his lecture[1] about the revaluation of the Trivium — that is the first three of the seven Liberal Arts — as against the Quadrivium. Now the Trivium was concerned with what we would call the arts of expression, and he said that some people look at Renaissance humanism as an upward valuation of these three Liberal Arts against the four more scientific ones that constituted the Quadrivium. It is true that Donne was what might loosely be called a humanist in that respect. He knew how to write, he knew how to argue and he knew how to persuade. And those were the main purposes of the Trivium. But he also knew a lot of things that belonged to the Quadrivium; he knew about number, he knew about geometry, he knew about astronomy and he knew about music; he knew about science as it was then conceived. He was early interested in Galileo. There's no doubt that he was concerned about the fate of Giordano Bruno, who was burnt for the heresy of suggesting that there were plural worlds, and other, perhaps populated, planets in the universe. He was interested in Kepler, the great

---

1 "The Renaissance — Period or Movement?"; *Background to the English Renaissance.* Gray-Mills.

astronomer, whose thought really came out of the idea of musical relationships in the creation; all these people were certainly of concern to him.

He was interested in Copernicus, as most people were — in fact the English were among the earliest people to be interested in Copernicus. He was also interested in the New World on this Earth, as well as those in the heavens. At one time when he was looking for a job he applied for the post of secretary with the Virginia Company and might very well have got it and gone to Virginia. There is something to be said for the view that, although Donne was a humanist in the sense that he was concerned with the revolution in the Arts of the Trivium, he was also interested in science; the new science as well as the old science, the science he had learned under the normal university system when he was at Oxford, though he did not of course take a degree.

He knew other humanist works. He knew, for example, the works of Montaigne, with his general relativism about the moral life, about his interesting libertarian speculations about sex, and the many other interesting things. Of course, the general sceptical cast of Montaigne's mind — very much part of the complex of what we think of as the Renaissance — was congenial to Donne also. And we must remember too that one of the effects of restoring the ancient authors in the sixteenth century was to give people a new picture of Ovid. Ovid, who had been treated throughout the Middle Ages as a kind of source of ancient morality and allegory, who had been turned into a religious poet, was suddenly seen for what he was, an extremely erotic poet. Marlowe had translated some of the *Amores,* and to the young Donne, writing his Elegies, which are certainly imitations of Ovid, Ovid was a source of myth, but also an erotic poet. The new learning released certain figures like Ovid (and part of Virgil too) from a sort of captivity they had been in for many centuries, when they had been used for purposes which would have very much surprised them.

So he knew this new way of doing things, but, as I say, he also knew the old way of doing things. He was very familiar with the old ways of knowing, and this is the important thing to remember. No matter how modern you want to make Donne seem, you've also go to see him as medieval. He knew about "disputation," he knew the scholastic philosphers well; he very often used St. Thomas Aquinas. And all these medieval aspects of Donne are just as important as the new things.

You see, at this time, if you were interested in science, you were bound to be interested in it in a medieval way. As Professor Gombrich said, the great movement of thought in science did not really come till after Donne's time; it is a seventeenth-century matter. No matter what he may have thought about Copernicus and the new philosophy, he certainly thought about it with a mind that had been trained in medieval methods. So also with the law; he was trained in law and his poems are full of allusions to recondite aspects of law; so with philosophy, theology and so on. I shall illustrate this later. What I'm really saying is that if you want to make Donne a Renaissance man, which is a very doubtful sort of concept anyway, you have to remember that to be a Renaissance man meant not only to be a modern, one of the precursors — as some of the historians Professor Gombrich talked about thought of the Renaissance man as being — not only one of the precursors of the moderns, but also one of the inheritors of the medieval.

That's a peculiar point you get to if you start thinking of a particular age as being a critical epoch; that the more you study it the more you see that as well as being very new in some respects, it is very old in others. This is exactly why scholarship is always pushing the Renaissance back, back to the twelfth century, for example. If you begin to look for signs of a stirring of a modern sort, then you are forced to abandon these very simple formulae.

However, I'm not going to get into the question of what the Renaissance was, or whether there was one, or whether it was just a "Renascence." The fact to remember is that, if we all assume for the moment there was one, the English version of it, the English Renaissance, came extremely late. There was a flurry of humanist scholarship at the Court of Henry VIII, but, for the most part, the English of the earlier part of the sixteenth century were too concerned in other matters to worry about having the sort of cultural rebirth that had happened already in Italy, notably, and in France. I think it is important to get this fact across, and I think we might do it quite simply by comparing a few dates:

Leonardo da Vinci ("Renaissance")	1452-1519
Michelangelo ("Mannerist")	1475-1564
Edmund Spenser	b. 1552 (The Shepheardes Calender, 1579)
Shakespeare and Marlowe	b. 1564
Donne and Ben Jonson	b. 1572
Rubens ("Baroque")	1577-1640
Bernini ("Baroque")	1598-1680

The man who typifies the "Renaissance Man" in most people's minds is Leonardo. Michelangelo, who is also connected by most people with the Renaissance, is called "Mannerist" by the art historians; that is to say, he is already past the Renaissance stage. Michelangelo died eight years before Donne was born. Rubens is the first really great artist to make his mark in England, but he and Bernini, the Italian artist who is largely responsible for what Rome looks like, are down in the book as "baroque" artists. So that by the time we get to Donne (1572-1631), the Renaissance had been "going on" for one hundred and twenty years before he was born, a lot more than that, in fact. If we put the beginning back to Petrarch, as Professor Gombrich did, then, of course, it had been going on for two hundred years. Now this will show you how very late the English Renaissance was. Even Spenser, who everybody thought of at the time as the great poet of the English Renaissance, was born as late as 1552 and the *Shepheardes Calender,* famous as a kind of manifesto of the new English poetry, was published in 1579 (one of those dates like 1066, or 1798).

The modern poets on whom Spenser depended were Ariosto and Tasso mostly, though partly on the French as well, and some of these were working quite far back in the sixteenth century. If you think of other English poets, they were all born later, including Jonson, the first great English classicist, which is, of course, part of the whole idea of the Renaissance; to restore the values of the ancient civilization. This is a crude indication to give you some idea of the belatedness, and then the extraordinary outburst, of English poetry in the last years of the reign of Elizabeth. This is well treated in C.S. Lewis's volume in the *Oxford History, English Literature in the Sixteenth Century,* where he distinguishes between "drab" and "golden" literature. He has a very good chapter on Donne, whom he doesn't like very much because he is a Spenser man really. Spenser, the "Prince of Poets" in his time, is doing exactly what Renaissance poets are meant to do because the Renaissance, of course, was a very nationalistic movement. You had to have your own vernacular poet who was going to be in the same class as Virgil. That is what Spenser was trying to do. He was trying to write an Epic. He is really, of all the people I have mentioned, the only one who had by this narrow definition straightforward Renaissance ambitions; the worship of an Empress, which has all kinds of political undertones, and so on. Shakespeare is a very extraordinary figure who resembles Donne only in one way, and that is that as he got to his mature phase, he had a colloquial, but complex way of registering passion which similarly distinguishes Donne from other poets of his time.

Marlowe, of course, died young, but he is, I think, one of the great pioneers (especially in the erotic poetry that he wrote) who did loosen things up. The fashionable poetry of the 1590's was erotic poetry in the Marlowe manner.

Satires, too, are very important because they were supposed to be written very roughly. This was a mistake, because people thought that the word "satire" had something to do with the word "satyr" so satires were supposed to involve wild men coming from the wood and lashing the follies and the sins of the town and so on, and not being able to speak very well. Therefore they wrote the satires very roughly, and so did Donne, and even when he imitates Horace he does it in a specially rough, harsh way. The word "harsh" is important for Donne. He said of himself, "I sing not, siren-like, to tempt; for I/Am harsh;".[1] This "harshness," though it is by no means uniform, is one of the important qualities of his tone. (Satires, incidentally, got so outrageous they were suppressed in 1598 by the Bishop of London, who had censorship rights on published books.)

The other fashionable form at the time, or one of them, was the sonnet. The Petrarchan sonnet was amorous in theme and you'll find some of the finest examples are Shakespeare's, though they are not wholly characteristic. The themes of Petrarchan sonnets are very often the themes of Donne's poems. That is a point on which Smith is very interesting.[2] But they are absolutely changed in tone; treated with irony sometimes; sometimes taken with a kind of over-seriousness which is comic. So that it is common to say that Donne was an anti-Petrarchist.

The other great vogue of the 1590's was pastoral poetry. This may be difficult for us to understand. People had developed a great passion for the simplicities of country life and the countryside. This is consistent, I think, with the sudden growth of London into a great city, which occurred to a great extent at this time. Sometimes it is used very subtly on the principle enunciated by Professor Empson – that you can say anything you need about complicated people by a close study of simple people – as a general basis of the Pastoral.[3] But sometimes it's really very trivial. The vogue may be illustrated by reference to a book called *England's Helicon,* that came out in 1601, a very popular anthology. As, one may imagine, the *Oxford Book of English Verse* was a few years ago, so *England's Helicon* was in 1601. In that book some poems are actually rewritten and converted into Pastorals. However, Donne had very little do do with that. Here and there in a commissioned poem he does a little bit of Pastoral, but, on the whole, the country did not interest him. He often refers to it as a place it is very easy to be bored in. "Meet mee at London, then," he says in one of his poems,[4] "that's where I'll be myself," he implies. And "Countrey ants" and that kind of thing are of no interest to him. He is interested in the life of the city: the life possible to a fairly well-off young

1 *Letter to Mr. S.B.* lines 9/10.
2 A.J. Smith. *Donne: Songs and Sonnets.* London, 1964.
3 W. Empson. *Some Versions of Pastoral.* London 1935.
4 *The Blossom* . Line 33.

man at the Inns of Court; a "great visitor of ladies"; a man who used to play a great deal, as we learn from fellow students; a hard-working student who sometimes worked five hours before ten o'clock in the morning and then spent the rest of the day enjoying himself. He was a city man and also very much, I think, a city poet.

And that brings one to a consideration of the sort of people he was writing for. He was certainly not writing as a professional poet. There were, roughly speaking, two sorts of professional poet in Elizabethan London. One was a playwright; these were people who worked, as Shakespeare did in his youth, and Marlowe, for theatre managers like Henslowe, the notorious Henslowe who paid so little and go so much work out of his playwrights. That was a very undignified way of making a living. The other sort found themselves a patron, someone like the countess of Bedford for whom Donne did write later when he was short of money, or it might be Sidney or his famous sister, and there were many others.

Poets were not very generously supported. The Queen was a skinflint; Spenser thought he was going to get a very large pension for *The Faerie Queene*, but he didn't. She liked people to write for her, but she didn't like paying them for doing so. The professionals aside, there were large numbers of what you might call gentlemen poets, amateurs, and this is the group into which the young Donne has to be placed. These people, like Sidney, felt that it was ungentlemanly to publish things. If you wanted to preserve your amateur status you did not publish, you merely circulated poems in manuscript. And this, in fact, is what he did. But it was impossible to say how large was the circle of people with access to his manuscripts; there's nothing to stop other people from copying them, and as other people got copies these bred very many other copies, so there are many manuscripts of Donne. So perhaps he was read more widely than it is usual to say. But in the first instance he was certainly read by friends, by fellow students, by young men in their twenties perhaps; that means, of course, people like Edward Herbert, George Herbert's elder brother, who was himself very interested in "harsh" poetry, and others of that sort, some of whom remained friends with Donne. We have letters he wrote to them much later on in his life. But, you see, there would be no need for him in any circumstances to make himself very plain. If he wanted to write difficult poetry, there was nothing whatever to stop him.

And so the first characteristics of Donne's poetry that we should notice are these: firstly, it's a poetry of argument. This is very important, simply because if you don't follow the argument you can't possibly know what he's up to. Nearly all his poems contain quite complicated arguments: backtracking arguments, arguments that turn upon themselves and, sometimes, arguments that proceed by faulty logic. So arguments of logic — or pseudo-logic if you like — are the first characteristic. The second characteristic we could put generally under the name of hyperbole. Under this heading you would certainly want to be more specific. You would have to say, for example, that Donne was very interested in the figure which the rhetoricians called "catachresis" or "the clench" or, as we should now call it, "the conceit."

Now I will return to these terms. What does "conceit" mean? What does "wit" mean? And certainly all these things are going to be grouped together and called "wit" when we get to the end of the story. Then we should have to say that the poems are characteristically obscure; not all of them, but characteristically they are so. And that is partly the product of the convolutions of arguments and the extravagance of what I'd loosely call hyperbole, all this conceited and exaggerated writing. It's very important to understand that the obscurity of Donne is not like the obscurity of a modern poet, and I think this cannot be over-emphasized. The obscurity to *The Waste Land* is an obscurity that will never be diminished; it's a poem that is written deliberately in order to force you to collaborate in the production of the meaning, and a lot of modern poetry is like that. It has, as Eliot himself said, "the logic of imagination," not the "logic of concepts." So it's no good trying to follow the argument of *The Waste Land*, or trying to tell yourself the story of *The Waste Land*. The process was wholly different.

Now in Donne that was not so. The obscurity is an obscurity of reference; very often he refers to sciences with which you're not familiar — like alchemy. He refers to theological points on, for instance, the nature of angels, with which you are not familiar; he refers to legal doctrines which you don't know, and strings them together in amorous poetry in a very curious way. You see, he is never writing *about* alchemy, or *about* theology. He puts them in an argument where they've never been together before. Leaving aside what used to be textual obscurities now largely cleared up, the obscurity of Donne is now an obscurity of allusion and argument. And because a lot of people have now worked on Donne for a long time I think it's true to say that there isn't any poem by Donne which is now inexplicable, except possibly *Farewell to Love,* which is very difficult. (I shall award a small prize at the end of the course for anyone who can give a convincing reading of that poem in detail.)

But on the whole we know what Donne is talking about and in the age of good annotation there's absolutely no reason why we shouldn't all come to a proper understanding of it. So his obscurity is not the darkness, as it were, of *The Waste Land*; this is a mistake that was commonly made in early twentieth-century criticism of Donne, for reasons which are interesting but which I won't go into now.

Let me just say one more thing about all this, which is all, incidentally, related to "wit," that key word which we must try and explain at some point. The followers of Donne, the real disciples of Donne later in the century, Cleveland for example, were quite unable to sustain the density of argument, conceit and allusion to the extent that Donne does. In fact they specialized the whole thing in such a way that the wit narrowed its meaning and became simply a matter of conceited writing. So that Cleveland is famous for what Dryden called "Clevelandisms," catachreses which are absurd jokes really, having nothing of the density for which Donne is famous. There isn't any other poet who holds this particular position. All the others narrowed it and specialized it in one way or another.

I would like to consider a poem called *The Dreame.* I've chosen this because it isn't particularly violent or harsh and it isn't particularly obscure, but it does illustrate a good number of points which are important for Donne. Incidentally, if you can get into the habit of reading Donne aloud to yourself it's better, because reading often explains to you where certain stresses fall and what the meaning is, which you'd otherwise miss:

Deare love, for nothing lesse than thee
Would I have broke this happy dreame,
　　It was a theame
For reason, much too strong for phantasie,
Therefore thou wakd'st me wisely; yet
My dreame thou brok'st not, but continued'st it,
Thou art so truth, that thoughts of thee suffice,
To make dreames truths; and fables histories;
Enter these armes, for since thou thought'st it best,
Not to dreame all my dreame, let's act the rest.

As lightning, or a Taper's light,
Thine eyes, and not thy noise wak'd mee;
　　Yet I thought thee
(For thou lovest truth) an Angell, at first sight,
But when I saw thou sawest my heart,
And knew'st my thoughts, beyond an Angel's art,
When thou knew'st what I dreamt, when thou knew'st when
Excesse of joy would wake me, and cam'st then,
I must confesse, it could not chuse but bee
Prophane, to thinke thee any thing but thee

Comming and staying show'd thee, thee,
But rising makes me doubt, that now,
   Thou art not thou.
That love is weake, where feare's as strong as hee;
'Tis not all spirit, pure and brave,
If mixture it of *Feare, Shame, Honor,* have.
Perchance as torches which must ready bee,
Men light and put out, so thou deal'st with mee,
Thou cam'st to kindle, goest to come; Then I
Will dreame that hope againe, but else would die.

Now, the topic of that poem is a familiar one. It's not an invention of Donne's, but a common theme in Renaissance poetry in several languages. The theme is of a man dreaming of a girl and waking up to find her standing by his bedside. You don't have to imagine, and on the other hand you don't have to "dis-imagine," an autobiographical situation for this poem. It is, if you like, an exercise on a topic, as are a great many Renaissance poems.

Let's look at the stanza of the poem. It's unique, with the short third line exactly repeated throughout the three ten-line stanzas. Now this again is very typical of Donne. He liked to set himself a rather difficult stanza the first time round and then to shape the argument of the poem as to match that stanza exactly repeated throughout the three ten-line stanzas. This again is difficulty overcome; you set yourself a stanza as difficult as this — he set himself more difficult ones, actually — and then keep a tight, complex argument flowing through it.

The next point we should note is, indeed, argument. The poem takes place in three stages: first he wakes and sees the woman; then he explains his pleasure at her being there; and finally she leaves, and he expresses his displeasure at that. That's another characteristic setting. A poem like *The Flea,* for example, has exactly the same shape. The lovers in bed together find a flea in the bed; they look at the flea in the first stanza; in the second stanza he says don't kill it and gives reasons for not doing so; and in the third stanza she kills it and he gives reasons for not caring. That's a very typical movement of a Donne poem. Now here we have him waking up and addressing the woman. Let me very crudely say where the allusions that make for obscurity in this poem go:

   It was a theame
For reason, much too strong for phantasie,

He's saying it was good to wake up, because what I was dreaming about was you, and that's to say that the theme was too good for pure fantasy and needs

the daylight reason.

Now here is the simple psychology of the time, which held that the imagination, or fantasy, or fancy — they synonymised the words then — continually produces images, but that when you are awake, and sane, and sober, these images are all kept in check by the reports of the outside world coming in through the senses. But when you are asleep or mad or drunk (or sometimes, they would add, a poet), then you close off the outer world altogether and your fantasy goes on operating, sending things up to the higher powers of your mind, uncensored. You remember the line in *Midsummer Night's Dream,* "The lunatic, the lover, and the poet" (5.1.2-22). Consequently dreams are the normal products of the fantasy, or the imagination, uncensored by information that comes in by the senses. "It was a theame/For reason, much too strong for phantasie," — what he's really saying is that it was right to get this theme out of the dream into daylight reason. Then, "Thou art so truth," or as some texts say, "Thou art so true." I think "truth" is very Donne-like. I prefer it. He goes on to argue, you see, that thoughts of her actually constitute the truth and make dreams come true — though of course they begin as lies — and they will turn fables into history. She gives Truth itself and converts fantasy into truth.

Then the second stanza turns on a reference to the doctrine of angels — if you like, to angelology — because, he says, when you first came in I thought you were an angel,

But when I saw thou sawest my heart,

And knew'st my thoughts, beyond an Angel's art,

and then he says:

. . . it could not chuse but bee

Prophane, to thinke thee any thing but thee.

That's a scholastic doctrine about angels. Angels do not have the power to see into the hearts of men, only God has that power. Consequently this is a rather daring theological joke. You can't be an angel; the only thing you could be, if you weren't yourself, is God. That, crudely, is what the last lines mean.

Then the final stanza. He thinks that she's gone away out of cowardice, or shame, or something of this kind, and he attacks all those qualities as he very often does in the *Songs and Sonnets: Feare, Shame, Honor.* "Honour" is nearly always in Donne a word spoken with a sneer, because it always has to do, in relation to women anyway, with chastity, and he was in this sense a "naturalist." He believed that people, if they lived naturally, would not concern themselves with fantasies like shame and honour; that they are all bred by custom; that they've no place in natural law, but are simply human inventions.

This doctrine of naturalism is something which he has in common with

Montaigne. Read the great essay of Montaigne, *Upon Certain Verses of Virgil*. It's not a very promising title, but the essay is about everything, really, and about naturalism too; it's about the way in which humanity have constricted their lives by unnecessary laws and customs, and "honour" would be one of them. He puts in that argument and then ends, surprisingly, with a quite homely figure: that perhaps she's gone and is going to come back, and perhaps she paid this visit just as people, if they're going to need a torch in a hurry, light it and put it out so that they can light it again quickly next time round. So he's quite capable in the same poem of referring to the doctrine of angelic perception in relation to divine perception, and then of having this quite homely figure of the torch at the end.

So here you have it: argument, certainly hyperbole in the general sense in which I have used it — that would account for the figure of the angels — and then the touch of naturalism and the homely conclusion. This is also, incidentally, a very musical poem, which is not always true of Donne.

IV

DONNE: LECTURE TWO

FRANK KERMODE

One of the words that is frequently used in connection with Donne is "wit." A lot of other words are used of him too, but the word "wit" and the word "conceit" are words which constantly come up. I haven't myself, you may have noticed, used the word "Metaphysical"; it's a purely historical description of a certain kind of poetry and it doesn't really mean anything. It was originally a sneer, in fact. Many words that stick are sneers, like "Baroque," or "Tory," but people adopt them and this kind of poetry just got called "Metaphysical"; but don't let that mislead you into thinking that it is *about* metaphysical problems. This mistake is sometimes made and I think it accounts for wrong readings of Donne.

The word "wit" is more important. In Elizabethan usage, or early seventeenth-century usage, "wit" did not have quite the specialized sense that we've given it since. It meant intellect, the operation of the mind; we still have the expression "he has his wits about him." "Wit" was understanding, if you like, and this rather specialized use of it was contained in the word at that time; but it had larger connotations and the reason why it had larger connotations is quite an interesting one, I think. It was felt that the best evidence of mental power was the power to compare unlike things. This was an idea that goes back as far as Aristotle. So the yoking together by violence of "heterogeneous ideas"[1] was a proof of genius.

We have to think of people living in a very different intellectual world from later ones, one where analogy — which we are taught to mistrust because analogies always break down and so are disproved — where analogy was considered a very powerful instrument of reasoning. So the ability to bring together two ideas or objects or thoughts that had never been brought together before was evidence of a very high power of intellect, or "ingenium" as they would say, using the Latin word. So when Elizabethan friends of Donne said he was a "witty poet" they meant something wholly commendatory. Later this idea changed, so that by the middle of the seventeenth century you have the notion that wit must be controlled by judgement or it's just a kind of madness.

From the very beginning, in Donne's own day, you have Ben Jonson, his friend and a professional poet, saying that he would perish for want of being understood. But also that "he was the first poet in the world in some things."[2] Now later on people went right off Donne and his followers, and this is reflected in a different notion of wit. Dryden, for example, began his career as a witty, metaphysical type of poet, but later used the word "metaphysical" as a sneer and said of the poet that he now condemned that he was a better Wit, but not a better Poet, than the people of his own time. So the idea of wit in the old sense became divorced from that of poetry. "Strong lines," which was a fashionable phrase used very often in the early seventeenth century to describe the sort of writing that Donne did, became a term of reprobation and not of approval. Even Walton, Donne's friend and biographer, spoke against the "strong lines now in fashion." And by the time we get to the mature Dryden, people had rather given this up. Donne's last follower of any consequence, Cowley, has a poem called *An Ode on Wit* in which you can see what the art of wit had become. It had become rather a kind of architectural principle in a poem, something that held the poem together and not one that exploded it with all kinds of metaphors.

A "conceit" — that's another difficult word — was nearly the same word as "concept" and was so used in Elizabethan English. If you spoke of someone's "conceit" you wouldn't be speaking, as you would now, of his vanity, but you would mean some idea he had got into his head. But this word again became specialized, just as "wit" did, and a "conceit" becomes an evidence of that power to bring together the heterogeneous, and therefore a proof of wit. So

---

1 S. Johnson: "Life of Cowley" in *Lives of the Poets* (1779-1781) — "The most heterogeneous ideas are yoked by violence together."
2 *Conversations with Drummond. Works.* Oxford 1925, ed. C.H. Herford and J. Simpson. Vol. 1, pp. 135 and 138.

conceit in that sense is really nothing much more than a rather striking metaphor, a surprising metaphor. Now, you'll find surprising metaphors in all poetry, in Tennyson for example, and no-one ever calls him a "conceited" or a "metaphysical" poet. The density or concentration of such kinds of metaphor helps to identify this kind of poetry. I don't for a moment mean there are lots of poets like Donne. I think there was no school of Donne, for example. That would be a very misleading thing to say. There were poets of wit, some of them religious and some of them secular.

The great religious poets of the period following Donne were Herbert and Vaughan, and I suppose the great secular poet of that period was Marvell. They all have this quality of wit in common with Donne, but they do not have in common with him, any of them, this quality of harshness. The people who did have that, such as Cleveland, we now tend to think of, on the whole, as bad poets. It took a long time to rescue Donne from that kind of condemnation and the story of how it was done is a very interesting one, but it's too long to tell.

People at various periods liked him. Coleridge liked him. He liked him because he gave him a brisk intellectual challenge and he recommends, almost as a school exercise, reading some of the tougher poems as a mind trainer. But, as I said before, it took a long time before Donne was restored to favour. By the end of the nineteenth century it was fashionable to like Donne — George Eliot liked Donne, for example. But there was no text worth having till 1912 and after that it became possible to know exactly what he was talking about and, therefore, to estimate more accurately the degree to which he tortured his metaphors and the true far-fetchedness of his conceits, which had sometimes hitherto been obscured by lack of understanding or bad texts. Now I wanted to say these few introductory words about the words "wit" and "conceit" before going back to some of the *Songs and Sonnets.*

Let me say that I don't, myself, attach any significance to the division of the *Songs and Sonnets* in Dame Helen Gardner's edition into youthful libertine poems and serious later poems. Not that I think they were all written at the same time, or that I think some are not more serious than others, but you cannot show this. I think it's a waste of time to try to elaborate the biography of Donne by describing a series of love affairs culminating in his marriage, and that sort of thing. For that reason I also have a great deal of difficulty believing either Grierson or Dame Helen Gardner or anyone else when they tell me that you can extract from the poems a consistent "love philosophy," sometimes very grandly stated. You can never do this with a poem by Donne simply because he's always alluding to bodies of learning, either religious or philosophical, or scientific or pseudo-scientific, and to say that, for example, in *The Extasie,* a poem I'll have to talk about a bit more, he gives a kind of quintessence of his views on sexual. love, seems to me almost meaningless. Therefore I think it's wrong to believe he must have written the *Nocturnall Upon S. Lucies Day*, for example, when he was in France, when he thought his wife might be dead in childbirth, and he was saying there's nothing left for me except to become a parson and hope to meet her again in heaven. That seems to me an extraordinary way to cheapen the poem, although Professor Empson thinks that I couldn't say that unless I secretly thought that Donne was rather a fraud, because he believes the poem has that kind of pressure behind it — which of course I admit; it's a very great poem, the greatest of Donne's poems — and must be about something real and not just fiction.

Well again, of course, it depends upon what you mean by real and fiction — I'd never dream of denying that. I simply say that to talk about that poem and try to relate it to Lucy, Countess of Bedford, or whoever it is that people do, seems to me just a way of escaping the poem. There's plenty going on in the poem without bringing all this stuff in from outside. So I would say your business although of course you're perfectly free to contest this view of how to do it — your business is to understand what goes on inside the poem rather than slot it into some purely speculative biography.

But that said, let's go to the poems which I said we would look at. *Love's Alchymie* is the first of them. I simply want to illustrate the points that I was trying to make before. I'm sorry to be repetitive, but it is, I think, important to know how to read the poems.

Some that have deeper digg'd loves Myne then I,
Say, where his centrique happinesse doth lie:
    I have lov'd, and got, and told,
But should I love, get, tell, till I were old,
I should not finde that hidden mysterie;
    Oh, 'tis imposture all:
And as no chymique yet th'Elixar got
    But glorifies his pregnant pot,
    If by the way to him befall
Some odoriferous thing, or med'cinall,
    So, lovers dreame a rich and long delight,
    But get a winter-seeming summers night.

Our ease, our thrift, our honor, and our day,
Shall we, for this vaine Bubles shadow pay?
    Ends love in this, that my man

Can be as happy as I can; If he can
Endure the short scorne of a Bridegroomes play?
   That loving wretch that sweares,
'Tis not the bodies marry, but the mindes,
   Which he in her Angelique findes,
   Would sweare as justly, that he heares,
In that dayes rude hoarse minstralsey, the spheares.
   Hope not for minde in women; at their best
   Sweetnesse and wit, they are but *Mummy,* possest.

Now, you see, this is a rather sour poem, though a very witty one as well. In line three, of course, "told" means counted. The figure is that he's been trying to find out what the happiness of love consists of by digging in his mind and counting the takings, as it were, but even if he went on digging for ever he would not find that hidden mystery, namely the "centrique happinesse" of love, and he says it's all an imposture. But, he says, when alchemists are looking for the Elixir they never find it; nevertheless as they try to find it they make odd accidental discoveries and these are rather valuable. They find new kinds of scent and new kinds of medicine and so on. (This, incidentally, was quite a frequent justification for going on with alchemy. Although nobody actually brought the project off successfully they did find things on the way.) So instead of getting the real thing all you get are these substitutes which keep you going. In the same way lovers imagine that their love is a rich and long delight, but in fact it turns out to be a cold and short one; a "summer's night" for length, but a winter's night for warmth. You see how many different sorts of ideas are put into that one stanza.

And then he muses, why should we pay so much attention to this bubble love so that we give up our comfort, our money and our honour for it? What is it in the end when you come to it? — and here's an idea he shares with Montaigne in his essay *On Certain Verses of Virgil.* Montaigne professes to be surprised in that essay that, although his serving man has never read the great philosophers of love, like Plato, Ficino and all the rest of them, he seems, curiously enough, to get on just as well with women as his master. The idea is repeated here; all he's got to do is put up with the brief tedium of a bridegroom's role and he'll get just as much as his master does. And that gives him the idea of representing the revelry at a wedding as particularly tiresome. He says anybody who really thinks that the marriage is of the mind as well as the bodies, is as foolish as someone who would find in the rough music that attended such a wedding the music of the spheres.

Now this attack on women occurs very often in Donne and of course you have to forget about that, or say he was joking, if you want to make him out to be a wholly serious of philosopher on love. Actually, of course, he did both things:

Hope not for minde in women; at their best
Sweetnesse and wit, they are but *Mummy,* possest.

He's speaking of "Mummy" in the sense of an Egyptian mummy. What he means is, women are dead as mummies, though they have some sweetness as mummies have — they used powdered mummy to make scent with — but in so far as they have a mind they only have one in the way that a mummy is possessed by a spirit. That I take to be the meaning of "*Mummy,* possest." Curiously enough Dame Helen Gardner, who usually is not given to libertinism in interpretation, takes a broader view of it and thinks that "possest" here is sexual. But what he's saying, in the primary sense at any rate, is quite clear. Women are simply corpses with devils inside them and that's how they appear to be alive. There you see quite a large number of different figures fuel the rather misogynous argument of the poem.

When you've said that you've still got to explain why it's a good poem. It's not simply a good poem because it's got a lot of wit in it. It's a good poem because of the satisfactory quality of its movement. It's a very difficult thing to describe, isn't it? But notice again the unique stanza, a newly invented stanza, as far as I know not used anywhere else, exactly repeated in the second verse. Again there's this sense, which communicates itself always with Donne, of the sheer difficulty of getting his argument to fit such an unusual shape, and that is certainly part of the pleasure of reading him. Not only that he argues, but that he argues under conditions of self-imposed difficulty. Then there is, as so often in Donne, a line that can haunt you without reference to its sense, about "some odoriferous thing, or med'cinall," which has not got some tremendous argument in it, one of those things that sweeten the poem and make it seem that it isn't all a matter of clashing arguments, but also a matter of euphony.

The Valediction of Weeping I chose because it renders an opposite kind of feeling. This is one of the poems in which the love between a man and a woman is taken very seriously. It's about a parting, as its title implies, and it's again got a stanza which is regularly re-employed through the poem and which has its own "tone." It doesn't sound like any other of the poet's because of its difference of shape.

Let me powre forth
My teares before thy face, whil'st I stay here,
For thy face coines them, and thy stampe they beare,
And by this Mintage they are something worth,
For thus they bee
Pregnant of thee;

Fruits of much griefe they are, emblemes of more,
When a teare falls, that thou falls which it bore,
So thou and I are nothing then, when on a divers shore.

   On a round ball
A workeman that hath copies by, can lay
An Europe, Afrique, and an Asia,
And quickly make that, which was nothing, *All*,
    So doth each teare,
    Which thee doth weare,
A globe, yea world by that impression grow,
Till thy teares mixt with mine doe overflow
This world, by waters sent from thee, my heaven dissolved so.

   O more then Moone,
Draw not up seas to drown me in thy spheare,
Weepe me not dead, in thine arms, but forbeare
To teach the sea, which it may doe too soone;
    Let not the winde
    Example finde,
To doe me more harme, than it purposeth;
Since thou and I sigh one anothers breath,
Who e'r sighes most, is cruellest, and hasts the others death.

I think this is one of the most beautiful of the *Songs and Sonnets* with the lovely last stanza and its great invocation at the beginning — "O more then Moone" — but remember that it has to be justified by the argument that precedes it; it's not just an isolated cry. Typical of Donne, too, is the way the stanza falls apart a bit at the end. The end of a Donne poem is often not as strong as what goes on in the middle and he has some difficulty in bringing this off, I think. A good example of this is *The Good-Morrow,* a very famous poem with a rather limp ending.

The first figure here is one of "coinage." It's one he uses in other poems. It's sometimes said that it's possible to exaggerate the extent of the range of Donne's metaphors. C.S. Lewis in a famous essay (which used to be in W.R. Keast's collection, but I see that in the revised edition it's not there any more)[3] said that when you made a list of his metaphors, there weren't so many of them and

---

Seventeenth Century Poetry, ed. Wm. Keast.

Donne used them like a stage army, going round and round. Well, if that's so, Donne's stage army certainly includes "coinage." Here it is tears which are like coins because her face is reflected in them. He then develops it; this makes the tears valuable because they are "pregnant of thee." And then the word "pregnant" — to say of a coin that it is "pregnant" of the Queen who is stamped on it is a rather odd idea. This produces the notion of fruits, the idea that these tears are the fruits of grief; past grief and emblems of future grief. But still hanging on to the idea of her face being on the tear: "When a teare falls, that *thou* falls which it bore" — "thou" is a noun, "that image of thee" is what it means; "that" is demonstrative and "thou" is a noun. So, when we are separate he says, of course we're nothing because our images have disappeared from the tears.

Now, still working on this figure, he comes to think of how you can take an absolutely blank sphere and place maps on it and so make it a geographical sphere. So you can make nothing into everything: "nothing, *All*." Again there is an excessive play which you get, again in *A Nocturnall upon St. Lucie's Day*, or "*all/nothing*." These extremes somehow fascinated Donne. He returns to them in his theological works too. He's playing on the inconceivability of nothingness and the inconceivability of "allness," which is identified with God. But here it's a simpler figure — a blank globe, and then a globe with maps on it; *nothing* and then *all*.

So here's a rather extended simile. As a workman does that, he says, so each tear which wears you, that is to say on which you paint your image, is a globe and therefore a world, because of the impression of you upon it. Even in a poem of lamentation like this, there is all this argumentative pushing, pushing the idea harder and harder. He now imagines his tears mixing with hers. His tears have the image of her upon them, but her tears come and drown that world which his tears now constitute. She is his heaven; the heavens dissolve, floods come and the world — the tear which has her picture on it — is drowned by these floods.

Now, this is what is called far-fetched, isn't it? This is what Donne himself meant when speaking of "itchy outbreaks of far-fetched wit." And yet, of course, he is serious, the tone is deadly serious. This is what is so fascinating about Donne; and this is what gives rise to so many theories, like the famous theory of Eliot's, that Donne's thought was something which modified his sensibility; so that he thought and felt simultaneously. The idea that you could be extremely serious, as this poem tells you he is, and yet go in for this extraordinarily over-wrought figure of the tears, that is what made him distasteful to the late seventeenth and eighteenth centuries and, finally, what made him fashionable in the late nineteenth and twentieth centuries. A strange mix of tones, a rhetorical solemnity, which nevertheless does not prevent this rapid, strange movement of argument.

Notice the great invocation in the third stanza, "O more then Moone, Draw not up seas to drowne me in thy spheare." He's thinking of the moon's sphere, which controls the tides, and he's asking her, as she's "more then Moone," not to induce floods and not to weep him dead, because the sea and the wind may do that soon enough — and here again we're back in the Petrarchan mode in which the sighs and tears of the lover can be compared to tempests and great storms and so forth, and although Donne can sometimes make fun of that kind of thing, here he's using it perfectly seriously.

Now, what you have to understand about this, I think, is the complexity not only of the argument but of the tone of the poem. I don't think anyone can call it a trivial exercise, and yet it has the sort of tortuousness which we for a long time did not associate with poetry. For the best part of a century, people's tastes were unconsciously formed by Tennyson, for example. In Eliot's famous essay on "The Metaphysical Poets" which you certainly ought to read, not because it's right, I think, but because it's a great historical document, he does compare Donne with Tennyson and Browning. He quotes rather unfairly, choosing a bad bit of Browning and a rather dim bit of Tennyson, to explain what had happened to English poetry in the meantime. And what had happened was that there had been a "dissociation of sensibility." The ability to think and feel simultaneously had died out.

Eliot always had this view (though he modified it later) and he always dated it from the time of the Civil War. That was the war which, as it were, split or ruined England, and to get again that unified sensibility which he found in Donne was his whole aim in poetry. And indeed it was the stated aim of a great deal of modern poetry — to restore wit to feeling. In a way this is the expression of personal preference, rather than anything which can be said to have happened historically, and it's also a way of expressing what Eliot thought good modern poetry ought to be. It ought to be quite like Donne in some ways; it ought to be quite like Jacobean tragedy in some ways; it ought to be like certain nineteenth-century French poetry in some ways; all this comes together, of course, in Eliot's own poetry which tries to be all those things. But I mention it here, not because I think it is accurate, but because it is a way of describing the feeling we get from a poem like *A Valediction of Weeping* — of the extraordinary and, what was for a long time, unusual, complexity of the poem, mixed with elements which were not expected to be found together in a poem until Donne was revived.

Now let me say a word about *The Extasie*, because I think it would be wrong to shirk it. I won't read it because, to tell you the the truth, I don't like it very much. It's been singled out by both the Oxford editors, perhaps unfortunately, as a central poem, and there's no doubt that Helen Gardner's note on it is a very useful one, relating it to certain kinds of sixteenth-century love philosophies which, I've no doubt whatsoever, are invoked in the poem. You'll notice that it is written in quatrains, which is somewhat unusual for Donne, and I think this is one of the reaons why it's rather a dull poem. He's much better with a complicated stanza.

It starts off with a particularly grotesque scene, I think, of the sort that's called nowadays a "*locus amoenus.*" The word itself simply means a pleasant place, but through a mistake, characteristic of the scholarship of the time, the word *amoenus* was derived from *amor*, so the pleasant place really became a place where you made love. There was a conventional way of putting this into poems. You have a pleasant garden, a grassy bank, with violets and so forth. Donne puts all that in with his usual impetuousness. If you look at his friend, Lord Herbert of Cherbury's poem, a very beautiful poem, *An Ode upon a Question moved, Whether Love should Continue for Ever,* you'll see a full scale *locus amoenus*; or Sidney's poem, *In a Grove Most Rich of Shade.* But Donne can't wait to do all that — he just puts in a "Pregnant banke" and one violet and that's really all he finds time for.

And then he has an extraordinary figure of their hands. They're holding hands which are "cimented" with a "fast balme," which is sweat, of course. As you remember from *Othello* (2.1.250), perspiring palms were an indication of sexual warmth. So he doesn't try to make that very glamorous. And their eye-beams are "twisted" together to such a degree that their eyeballs look like beads hanging on them. This is the kind of grotesquerie in Donne that his followers unfortunately imitated rather than things like *A Valediction of Weeping.*

In the third stanza he says this is all we've done, as yet. We have inter-grafted our hands; "grafting" was a garden image, of course, and again there are sexual connotations. Gardeners were sometimes called "panders" because they inserted grafts into other plants. That's the only thing we've done, he says, and the only propagation we've gone in for is to get "babies" in one another's eyes. That is again a common figure in love poetry — the reflections lovers made in one another's eyes were called "babies."

Now I think there's a strong implication in that stanza — I don't know what you think — that this is a poem of seduction; that this is a poem, as Dryden said, in which Donne is trying to perplex "the minds of the fair sex with nice specu-lations of philosophy";[4] to talk people into being seduced by simply being

---

4 J. Dryden in *A Discourse concerning the Original and Progress of Satire.* 1693.

unintelligibly clever. However, this view is very hotly resisted. There are more views about this poem than about any other of Donne's and opinions vary very greatly from the candid view, to which I incline, of the French critic, Legouis,[5] who says it is a seduction poem, to the opposite view, a very extraordinary one by the American scholar, Potter, who says that it's a man talking to his wife.[6] I find that view very difficult to understand, as well as Dame Helen Gardner's view, which holds that in fact it isn't about sex at all, but about souls leaving their bodies and then returning to them. I think it's nothing of the sort, but that people have simply misunderstood. I think the "as yet" in that third stanza is particularly important. He means really that he isn't altogether content to leave things that way, as they lie "like sepulchrall statues."

And then he has the figure of the "Fate" between two armies. He says our souls have gone out to negotiate. "Negotiate" again suggests some sort of activity, though not military, which will happen quite soon, otherwise there's nothing to negotiate about. I think it's awfully difficult to read this poem as a simply abstract, straightforward exposition of a philosophy of love.

Then he imagines a spectator. He's got the souls out of the bodies. The bodies lie "like sepulchrall statues," like statues on tombs, and a conversation ensues, not really a conversation because the two souls are one, but a monologue, or so he argues. And then there is a very refined spectator standing near, who would hear what the souls said. The figure of "concoction" (st. 7) comes from physiology. This is what you do to your food. You "concoct," or digest, it and from it come more ethereal things called animal spirits, which circulate around your body, so in fact is purifies the food to a degree where it can support that part of yourself which is not physical. That's what he's saying here; the spectator is so refined by love.

Refining people by love is another great Renaissance-Platonic concept, expressed in Castiglione's *The Courtier*, and by other poets, including Spenser. The "Extasie," incidentally, simply means the "standing outside"; the souls standing outside the bodies. Being outside their bodies makes things simpler to understand, they understand the nature of their love; "Wee see by this, it was not sexe," — that's a very famous line because it is the first recorded occurrence in English of that abstract use of "sex." Before that it was really only used in the sense of distinguishing between men and women. Here it is used of the relationship between then. "It was not sexe" — our love was higher, as it were. Now we

---

5 P. Legouis. *Donne the Craftsman*. Paris 1928. pp.61-68, an introduction to Donne's *Poèmes Choisis*. Paris 1955. p.29.
6 G.R. Potter. "Donne's *Extasie*, Contra Legouis" *PQ* XV. 1936.

can see what caused it all, which we couldn't see before.

Then he puts forward an extremely complicated argument. If you have a single soul, that's made up of a mixture of things. But if you have a combined soul, like theirs, that soul is made up of pure single souls and therefore not subject to corruption. That's what the next few stanzas mean. I think that's a particularly low-keyed example of Donne doing that kind of conceit. It's a bit laborious and altogether below what we know he can do. We "are this new soule" and "no change can invade (line 48) us." In other words, everything's going to be fine. We have a union of souls, this really is a single soul, we have perfect union with each other.

Then line 49:

But O alas, so long, so farre
Our bodies why doe we forbeare?

and clearly the argument has absolutely changed. He has just been saying that their souls were one in this spiritual union and he's now going to argue that, nevertheless, they should not forbear their bodies. They are only a relatively insignificant part of us, we are "th' intelligences," that is to say, the angels who look after the orbit or the spheres of planets, and our bodies are the planets, the material things which the angelical intelligences look after. We ought to be grateful to them because without them we could not have been brought together.

In line 55, "Yeelded their forces, sense, to us" there is a difficulty. "Senses force" is one reading, "forces, sense" is another. In the end it really comes to the same idea — though "senses force" seems better really — the power of their senses, the senses of the body which apprehend the physical world. We mustn't think of them as dross, what's left over after the process of refinement, but as "allay," that's to say, alloy, something which when mixed with the souls makes the souls actually stronger, as alloy is used to strengthen gold. Bodies are necessary because souls must first imprint themselves on bodies before they can attain each other, just as heaven's influence, that is the influence of the stars, was held to work first by imprinting itself on the air. In the same way — "blood labours to beget/Spirits, as like soules as it can" — these are the animal spirits which I mentioned before, they hold together body and souls quite literally. They are the "subtile knot, which makes us man." And as you always need something physical for these spiritual effects to occur,

So must pure lovers soules descend
T'affections, and to faculties. . .

Passion needs the apparatus of the body, as it were; if not, the soul, the "great Prince," will simply lie in prison (st. 17). So let us turn to our bodies, he says (line 69). Now there you are, that's the line. Is he simply saying that we've been out here long enough debating, now let's get back to our bodies, or is he suggesting some other use for those "bodies"? So "Weake men on love reveal'd may looke" — that's another figure which he often uses, incidentally, — the notion that love is an abstract spiritual history, like religion, but that we learn from it as from the Bible, which is an actual physical book. Just as our love is abstract and mysterious, yet it can be revealed only by the use of the body which is its book. And he *then* comes back to the spectator and says: When we do make love — if I'm right about the poem — he'll not think it very different from what we are doing when we are simply having a spiritual union.

It's a very curious poem in many ways, I think. There's a sort of voyeur element in it which is even slightly disagreeable, I'd say. Anyway, I mention it, if only to say you can't really explain Donne's "love philosophy" from that and then work it out in the other poems.

I think I have said enough about the *Songs and Sonnets* to give you a general idea of what I think about them. We will look next at the *Elegies* and *Satyres,* I haven't said much about Donne's life; it seems foolish to spend time doing so when you can read about it anywhere. However, the *Elegies* and the *Satyres* do happen to be poems which we know he wrote when he was a young man, in the 1590's.

V

DONNE: LECTURE THREE

FRANK KERMODE

As I have said, I don't think you can construct a biography from Donne's poems, but some of them are certainly libertine poems. They are about sex, they are poems which clearly do advocate, or take the pose of advocating, extreme libertinism in sexual matters. So we get a picture of a young man at the Inns of Court leading a life (if we're willing to make simple biographical inferences) of a libertine, something which you'd expect to find in fashionable London of the 1590's.

You'd certainly expect to find people writing libertine poems; there were a good many of them. But before you get the idea that Donne was devoted to libertine poetry and speculation I would ask you to remember that among his *Satyres* there is a very important one, namely the third, which is a very religious poem. So you have the contradiction of a libertine and a religious poet in the same body, so to speak.

This isn't a contradiction of any significance, I think. Religion was a much more pressing matter in this period than in our own. It was a matter of course, in which everyone had to take a position; there were no atheists at this time. When the word was used, of Marlowe, it did not mean what we now mean. It was not used in the etymological sense of the word. If you called someone an atheist you meant he was a loose liver, a blasphemer and that kind of thing. Marlowe's atheism is described in what is known as the Baines note, and really consists of saying rude things about the Christian religion and not in saying that there was no God.

So people were serious about religion. And some people had to be very serious about it, if they were Roman Catholics as Donne was. The reason for this was that it was impossible to separate religion from politics and the security of society in the Elizabethan period. Remember that Elizabeth's reign followed on her sister Mary's, which was extremely Catholic, and that followed on their brother Edward's, which was extremely Protestant. Moreover Elizabeth had a very shaky religious settlement made sometime after she ascended to the throne and this was not popular really anywhere.

It certainly wasn't popular with the Roman Catholics. Conformity was required. You had to go to church. That is to say you had to go to the Church of England, and if you didn't go you had to suffer fines. People could be ruined by such fines. But if you were militantly Catholic, as Donne's family were – they were proclaimed Roman Catholics – then you were in much more serious trouble, not so much because they resented your opinions as that you were a political enemy. You were a political enemy because of the protracted war, usually cold, but at times, hot, against Spain, and Spain, of course, was a Catholic imperialist country. The two countries were fighting really for control of trade and, in fact, it was a great imperialist conflict.

If you took the side of the Spanish, as some English Catholics did – and, of course, all this came to a head in 1605 – then you clearly were an enemy of the State. For this reason Donne's brother was imprisoned for harbouring a Jesuit priest. There were Jesuit missions of great courage and pertinacity which exercised Donne's imagination of great deal. They came over from Europe and did many illegal things which were punishable by death. Donne's brother harboured such a priest, was caught, and the priest was executed as a traitor with all the horrors that that always involved. Donne's brother was put in prison, where he caught the plague and died; so what with that and his impeccable Catholic ancestry (which included Sir Thomas More and Jasper Heywood), Donne was very strongly rooted on the Catholic side.

However, he always distrusted the Jesuit missions as far as one can tell. He thought the Jesuits were seeking martyrdom, which seemed to him an improper thing to do. He wrote a book called *Pseudo-Martyr* in which he discusses this. And although he belonged to the old faith for some time, he was under great pressure to change it. The pressure arose from the lack of opportunities even for a clever recusant man like him in State employment, if he remained a Catholic. All this is familiar, but I'm trying to explain why it should be that a bright young man of twenty-two, in 1594, should have written the *Third Satyre* as well as perhaps the libertine elegies.

The *Third Satyre* is really about the need to choose a religion and the difficulties of doing so. I'll discuss the details soon. The point I'm making now, though, is that it would have been impossible for a man in his position not to have taken a profound interest in religion, even if he wasn't essentially a religious person, as indeed he quite clearly was. That will emerge also from the *Third Satyre*, because, he himself says, as Walton said about him, that he did spend a great deal of time in these years minutely examining the case for and against the Catholic Church.

He'd be unlikely, I think, to accept a good deal of the Anglican propaganda that was put about at the time concerning the antiquity of the two Churches, suggesting that the Church of England was, in fact the true and primitive Catholic Church and the Church of Rome a later upstart. It was a very brilliant propaganda trick that was contrived during the reign of Elizabeth. But he was obviously impressed much more by the philosophical treatment of the subject by Hooker in the *Laws of Ecclesiastical Polity* and in certain earlier works.

So here we have this curious picture of a young man with his way to make at the Inns of Court, deeply concerned with religion and writing the libertine *Elegies*. With that word of introduction, let me say something about the *Elegies*. The best treatment of them in a book, I think, is J.B. Leishman's *The Monarch of Wit*. It is a long, rambling rather strange book, but a rather delightful book, too. The treatment of the relationship of Donne to Ovid is, I think, a classic of the subject, so you ought to read that.

Ovid was a very important poet for this period. He was one of the Roman poets who had survived and kept on being read all through. He was not a Renaissance rediscovery in that sense. What *was* a rediscovery was to take Ovid straight. To take, for example, his *Art of Love* not as an allegory about the quest of the soul for God but as what he said it was, namely a handbook on seduction. And the love poems, or *Amores,* were poems of the same sort: libertine poems about love. These were often called Elegies, and Donne imitates these Ovidian Elegies. He uses them as a model for naturalistic love poetry. Ovid was famous for his mellifluousness as well as for his conceitedness but not for his harshness, and the *Elegies* have a kind of energy or violence which is not characteristic of Ovid.

They're also much more various than I've suggested. There are elegies of various different kinds. Some of them – for example *The Anagram* – are really a series of jokes about a deformed mistress. It's a favourite theme of the time; an elaborate way of saying how ugly somebody else's mistress was:

Though all her parts be not in th'usuall place,
She, hath yet an Anagram of a good face.

This is the sort of fairly insulting joke which fitted the poem's tone. Very different is the serious tone of the Elegy *On his Mistris,* which begins with the famous invocation to a mistress not to accompany him, not to dress up as a page and follow him on a dangerous journey:

By our first strange and fatall interview,
By all desires which thereof did ensue,
By our long sterving hopes, by that remorse
Which my words masculine perswasive force
Begot in thee, and by the memory
Of hurts which spies and rivalls threatened mee,
I calmely beg; but by thy parents wrath,
By all paines which want and divorcement hath,
I conjure thee; and all those oathes which I
And thou have sworne, to seal joint constancie,
Here I unsweare, and over-sweare them thus:
Thou shalt not love by meanes so dangerous.

Now this is a little dramatic monologue. We're not required to imagine that Donne himself was about to go on a dangerous journey and that a girl was proposing to dress up as a man and follow him, but, again, it's a set piece in a way. It has that note of urgency and passion that he could achieve and which he accommodates in the *Elegies* together with the more guttersnipe writing that you get in a poem like *The Anagram.*

However, the two poems that I asked you to look at particularly were the Elegies *Natures Lay Ideot* and *To His Mistris going to Bed.* (The former is called *Tutelage* by Helen Gardner.) "Natures Lay Ideot, I taught thee to love." Now here's a very simple idea — again a dramatic situation. A man, presumably racked with jealousy, but more with anger, in that he has actually managed to seduce a girl — a very stupid girl who knew nothing about love — then sees her marry someone else. As it were, having prepared her for sexual pleasure, he must let someone else take over when all the hard work has been done. This is a libertine theme, of course. What is notable about it is the vigour, the kind of mock hatred that he gets into it, particularly in the conclusion. (I won't read it all because it takes too much time.) The argument is that he taught her all there is to know about love. He goes on:

Thou art not by so many duties his,
That from the worlds Common having sever'd thee,
Inlaid thee, neither to be seene, nor see,

As mine: who have with amorous delicacies
Refin'd thee' into a blis-full paradise.
Thy graces and good words my creatures bee;
I planted knowledge and lifes tree in thee,
Which Oh, shall strangers taste? Must I alas
Frame and enamell Plate, and drinke in Glasse?
Chafe waxe for others seales? breake a colts force
And leave him then, beeing made a ready horse?

All this is very characteristic of the Donne you've already come to know; that is, it's got the note of passion or indignation, however unworthy, but it combines this with, and in fact expresses this with, a series of quite different figures. The most important is that he has created in the body of this girl an Eden of pleasure, a "paradise" of pleasure, which he can't resist developing to the point where he puts the Tree of Life and the Tree of Knowledge into the garden.

That's worth remembering as a very characteristic figure of the time. The idea of the body of a woman as a figure of Paradise was often used in English Renaissance poetry. But nobody else would do it in quite this way, nor on quite such an occasion as this. The sort of poet, Chapman for instance, who developed this figure — the beloved's body as Paradise — did it quite differently. Donne says: I made a Paradise but some other Adam has got in there, so to speak; and he develops it in this rather kinky manner. Then he develops that with the idea of taste, in line 27, giving rise to another figure; he has made an exquisite drinking vessel of plate, but somebody else drinks out of it while he has to use the common or garden glass. He "chafes" the wax, that is warms the wax — an extremely obscene figure this — where somebody else impresses the seal. And then, finally, this idea lends him to the idea of his having broken a horse and being left without a mount, though leaving someone else contentedly provided.

Well, that's the tone of Donne's libertinism, if you like; a bit raw, very forceful and very conceited. Very unlike Ovid, incidentally, who always had a kind of metropolitan smoothness that Donne doesn't have.

Take a poem like *To his Mistris going to Bed,* one of the most famous of the Elegies; a poem which was a little too much for the publisher in 1633. He left it out of Donne's poems because, presumably, it was too obscene. Several of the Elegies were left out on this ground — not published till after the Restoration, in fact — and there's an interesting issue here which I'll talk about when we come to the end of the poem. It arises from the fact that it existed for almost seventy years before it got into print. That means it survived in manuscript only, and as one scribe copies from another he always adds to the mistakes. The manuscript tradition splits into different directions and you get controverted readings, some-times important, sometimes not. In this poem, I think, you will see that the controverted reading at the end of the poem actually changes the tone of the whole poem, so it's a nice little exercise to choose between the two main alternatives.

Now this poem has a very simple idea. It's a poem about going to bed with someone with whom you've not been to bed before. This is proved by the fact that he addresses the woman as "you" in the first half and as "thee" in the second half, indicating a rapidly growing intimacy. In Elizabethan English — it's very important in Shakespeare — something like the modern French distinction between *tu* and *vous* was still employed. That alone will rule out the idiotic readings of this poem which suggest that it's addressed to a wife. Quite clearly — as Dame Helen says in her note — it's not a poem of that sort, it's a poem about a city madam of some kind, perhaps the wife of some rich city tradesman judging from the way she dresses. It's full of the usual sexual puns of the time; of

The foe oft-times, having a foe in sight,

Is tir'd with standing, though he never fight.

and then the later puns on dying — all the usual things you find in Shakespeare, in fact. Then there's a description of the woman undressing. If you try to imagine this as a real dramatic scene it would be very implausible wouldn't it? It's a poem, not an account of an actual scene.

Again, I won't dwell on the first 24 lines; I think they're pretty clear anyway. The famous passage in the poem begins at line 25:

Licence my roving hands, and let them goe,

Behind, before, above, between, below.

Oh my America, my new found lande,

My kingdome, safeliest when with one man man'd,

My myne of precious stones, my Emperee,

How blest am I in this discovering thee.

Here he uses this conceit of a newly discovered territory, an America, a new found land, hence the word "discovering" in line 30. But, curiously enough, everybody feels a change in the tone of the poem here, a kind of rapt quality comes into it. An authentic sense of sexual excitement enters the poem, which is why these lines are remembered and a lot of other conceits in the poem are forgotten.

The next one, for example:

To enter in these bonds is to be free,

Then where my hand is set my seal shall be.

It's a legal figure, "to enter in these bonds," but going into *these* bonds is different; it is to be free. Then, of course, again, it's the same obscene joke about seals which you get in the other poem about "Tutelage." Here, of course, the idea is of signing and sealing, setting your hand to something, and then setting your seal to it — the sexual implications are obvious.

Also characteristic is the infusion of a certain theological conceit into a poem; "Full nakedness, all joyes are due to thee." That's simple, and an understandable sentiment, but who except Donne would go on to enforce it by saying

As soules unbodied, bodies uncloth'd must bee

To taste whole joyes.

That is to say, you have to die and drop your body off, so to speak, before your soul can enjoy heaven and, in the same way, you have to take off your outer covering in order to taste bodily joys. Then there's an unsuccessful figure from Greek mythology (1.36): it wasn't Atlanta who threw the balls down in order to slow down her suitors, it was the suitors who threw down the balls to slow down Atlanta. He actually got that one wrong. Then, again, he's back to theology:

Like pictures, or like bookes gay coverings made

For laymen, are all women thus arraid;

Themselves are mystique books, which only wee

Whom their imputed grace will dignify

Must see reveal'd.

Now that is simple enough; he means that the clothing of women is like the ornate binding of a book. But women are mystic books, that is, books containing a quasi-religious mystery which we cannot understand except as we understand religious mysteries, namely by grace imputed to us by Christ. We only understand the mystery of women by grace, which is imputed to us by them. That will reveal it in the same sense that the Bible, for example, reveals religion. From there he moves to another figure which might strike us as being a bit out of court:

As liberally as to a midwife showe

Thy selfe; cast all, yea this white linnen hence.

Here is no pennance, much lesse innocence.

This is the disputed line. This is Helen Gardner's reading — "Here is no pennance, much lesse innocence." The other reading, which is just as strongly supported, is "There is no pennance due to innocence." Now there's been a great deal of extremely angry controversy about this. For my own part, I agree with Helen Gardner. It's saying that white stands for penance and white stands for innocence. You're clearly not in a condition of penance at the moment considering what you're doing and it's useless to pretend that you are innocent. It depends on the situation as you see it. If this is somebody else's wife, that's what he's saying — "Here is no pennance, much less innocence." But the other view is to impute to Donne a very strong view about sexual liberty. What you're doing is innocent, therefore you don't require to do any penance; get your "white linnen" off. You can see how this alters the poem.

The reading I gave makes this a cynical city sort of poem, does it not? More or less a casual love affair. It's useless to pretend (it's just a joke, really) that you should be wearing white, get it off. You're not penitent and you're not innocent. The other view is that what you're doing is innocent because all genuine sexual activity is admirable. Therefore it's inappropriate that you should be wearing white because that is the mark of penitence. You've got to take your pick.

At this point the poem comes to an end. But again one can see that what is distinguished about Donne is not the subject here but the variations of tone, and also the persistence of these quasi-learned figures from theology, from geography and so on, which don't have the effect of making it a dry crackle of wit, as with those of his successors, but which are perfectly consonant in Donne with a tone of authentic passion.

And that is what links the *Elegies* with the *Satyres* which are, as I say, equally of the 1590's. The satires were, in fact, a remarkable vogue in the 1590's. So much so, and so outrageous did they grow in tone at times, that the Bishop of London suppressed them in 1598. No more satires were allowed to be published. The vogue continued, in a way, by putting satire on the stage. Ben Jonson was particularly good at that. However, Donne, though among the earliest satirists, presumably never published his *Satyres*. He perhaps shared, and perhaps didn't, the mistaken view that satires were supposed to be spoken by rough men — Satyrs, in fact — who would come in from "nature" and look at the city and describe it.

The satire is the true urban form of poetry. It always confines itself to the crimes and misdemeanours of a rich urban society. Its characteristic topics are luxury, wickedness and women; women were given a very bad time in satire. The models behind them were ultimately derived from Horace — chatty, colloquial *sermones* as they were called, not "satyres" in the sense of having been spoken by a satyr — and the more explicit and fierce satires of Juvenal, with their condemnation of lust, luxury and greed. Donne certainly had a lot in common with these. He does imitate Horace quite correctly sometimes, but he employs a certain rough harshness of manner as appropriate to satire, that you don't find in Horace.

I asked you to read the *First Satyre* because it's more conventional. It's very much a London street scene of the 1590's. It's an attack by a supposedly serious man on the affectations of an absurd fop; a figure that gets on the stage in the plays of Ben Jonson a little later than this and remains in the English theatrical tradition for quite a long time after. It's not an easy poem and, again, it's quite a long one so I can't spend a lot of time on it. But it's worth working it out to make sure you understand the detail, which is really quite precise and interesting.

The picture is of a man being tempted out of his study by a foppish friend to go for a walk in the street. He knows what is going to happen and he tries to make the friend promise that he won't skip about, making a fool of himself and abandoning his companion while he pays court to rich and fashionable people. But, of course, he doesn't keep that promise and when they get into the street, which takes them 66 rather witty lines, this is what happens:

> He first of all
> Improvidently proud, creepes to the wall,
> And so imprison'd, and hem'd in by mee
> Sells for a little state his libertie;

Now, that means that as the man can't bear to concede a higher rank to his companion, he takes the inside position, because the people of higher rank went near the wall and *you* took all the dirt that came up from the gutters. However, having taken the socially superior position, he finds his movements very cramped; he can't skip about "to greet/Every fine silken painted foole we meet," – instead of that he must just ogle and make various disagreeable gestures; he "grins, smacks, shrugs," bowing across the street at people, running off to talk to them in the end.

> Now leaps he upright, joggs me, and cryes, "Do'you see
> Yonder well favour'd youth?". "Which?". "Oh, 'tis hee
> That dances so divinely"; "Oh", said I,
> "Stand still, must you dance here for company?".

Now that's the rather surly, common-sense man in contrast with this butterfly figure. Then there's the usual attack on tobacco:

> till one (which did excell
> Th'Indians, in drinking his tobacco well)
> Met us;

There were many attacks on tobacco in the period, not least because it was very expensive. It cost threepence for a little pipe if you went in a bought it at a tobacconist's. This is a time when a labourer earned a shilling a day, so you couldn't smoke very much tobacco unless you were rich. It was a piece of conspicuous consumption which was much deplored and soon James I wrote a pamphlet against it. This is again very modish. Tobacco had only come in about twenty years earlier and the fashion is being attacked. So is the fashion of travel. The fop rushes off and bows deeply to someones who has travelled. Travel was a great joke. People went off, especially to France and Italy, and came back with all sorts of outlandish un-English habits and were much derided for doing so.

"Why? he hath travail'd"; "Long?". "No; but to me"
(Which understand none) "he doth seeme to be
Perfect French and Italian" I reply'd,
"So is the Poxe."

This is another piece of chauvinism, very common at the time. You always described syphilis as a thing that you got in France or Italy, never at home. And so he rushes off again, finally, to some courtesan, but is disappointed there and goes home. Not a very important poem, but a poem that does give you the sense of Donne in the London of that time, adopting yet another "persona," that of the solid man, the student, not really affected by all this folly. But, again, one feels this is only a pose.

That's what makes the *Third Satyre* so very extraordinary. The *Third Satyre* is not really like a satire at all and at the beginning it more or less says so. This is a very passionate meditation on religion; on the necessity to choose a religion, with all the difficulties that are in the way of choice and coming from a man of extremely sceptical temperament. By "sceptical" I mean something quite precise, not as we use the word now. "Sceptical" — lacking confidence in the power of the human mind, which after all is fallen, lacking power even in the reports of the senses. This is very characteristic of Donne, as we'll see in *The Anniversaries.*

But this sceptical characteristic is a good thing in a way; to doubt wisely, as he says in the poem, is good, but it doesn't exempt you from the absolute need to choose. Nor do the political pressures of the period. It was much easier to conform in Europe at this time where it was customary for a ruler to impose on his people, as it had been in England. They had been Protestants under Edward, Catholics under Mary and Protestants again under Elizabeth, and this, of course, was to carry on right through the seventeenth century (v. the *Vicar of Bray*).

Yet it was still necessary to choose. For Donne there was an additional necessity, which we mustn't forget, that he chose the Church of England because if he didn't he was going to get into serious trouble. He had already not taken his degree at Oxford because he was ineligible as a Catholic; he'd got into the Inns of Court, presumably under some undertaking that he was not a Catholic, but it was at this time that he was trying to work it all out, with a great temptation to work it out the right way from the worldly point of view — as indeed he did a few years after this in 1598 and got a very good job as Secretary to the Lord

Keeper, Sir Thomas Egerton, which he only lost through his own rash marriage. He had a spell in prison and never got a job again until he took orders in 1614 as a last resort, really, and then was pushed along quite quickly in the Church.

However, at this point in his life it was, clearly, a big decision. He could have a brilliant career or so it appeared, in the State Service, or none at all. He had some private means but not enough. So the worldly pressure to choose right was on him all the time – to choose the Church of England. It is very remarkable that he was able to write a poem like this that doesn't come down on any side. This confirms what he said himself in *Pseudo-Martyr*, that he "used no inordinate haste nor precipitation in binding my conscience to any locall Religion." And this poem was certainly written at a time when he was doing a great amount of reading in the controversy between the Church of Rome and the Church of England. He wrote this poem, almost certainly, in 1594. It is a very important poem. Without it I think you get a very unbalanced picture of Donne.

Look, for example, at line 5, and the following lines:

Is not our mistresse faire Religion,
As worthy of all our Soules devotion,
As vertue was to the first blinded age?
Are not heavens joyes as valiant to asswage
Lusts, as earths honour was to them? Alas,
As wee do them in meanes, shall they surpasse
Us in the end, and shall thy fathers spirit
Meete blinde Philosophers in heaven, whose merit
Of strict life may be' imputed faith, and heare
Thee, whom hee taught so easie wayes and neare
To follow, damn'd?

Now that's a very involved sentence. What he's saying is, shouldn't religion be as important to us as virtue was in the age before the Incarnation, the blinded age, the age of the pagan philosophers? Shouldn't the joys of heaven, of which we have assurance, be as strong to us, control our passions, as the desire for earthly honour did in the pagan world? This is a theme which St. Augustine deals with at great length in the *City of God*. The pagans led virtuous lives for the sake of earthly honour, but we have much greater inducement to lead virtuous lives in the hope of heavenly joys; our means are greater than theirs, but "shall they surpasse/Us in the end?" They do better than us in spite of our advantages. How would you like it if your father's spirit met blind philosophers – that is to say, again, philosophers of the blinded age (He's thinking for example of Aristotle, the author of the great *Nicomachean Ethics*) who is in heaven by virtue of his strict life? Not because of his faith, because he couldn't have faith, but his strict life is commensurate with faith and therefore he's in heaven. *They* got to heaven although their means for doing so were bad, and yet you don't, although your means are relatively easy and simple. You ought to be very afraid of this, he says; such a fear would be equivalent to great courage.

Then he goes on to talk about the sort of courage men have. They have courage to go to war; they have courage to go to sea in terrible, dangerous ships; to voyage into equatorial and arctic regions and so on. They are courageous enough to do all these things for gain. Can't they see that their true interests, their true gain, lie elsewhere? People will fight duels over absurdities, quarrels over mistresses, and yet they don't tackle their true enemies. Then he sets out their true enemies, in line 33 and the following lines, in unconventional order for us — the Devil, the World and Flesh. The devil first, then the world and, last, the flesh;

Flesh (it selfes death) and joyes which flesh can taste,
Thou lov'st; and thy faire goodly soule, which doth
Give this flesh power to taste joy, thou dost loath.

You ruin, or stain, the soul, which moves the body, for the sake of bodily pleasure. What you should be doing instead of yielding to these foes is seeking true religion.

Then he runs through the available alternatives. "Mirreus" is an adherent of the Church of Rome:

Thinking her unhous'd here, and fled from us,
Seekes her at Rome, there, because hee doth know
That shee was there a thousand yeares agoe. . .

"Mirreus" — Swift uses the anagram Mreo for the Church of Rome and that, latinized, would be Mirreus, and I think that's probably where that name comes from. What the other names mean nobody is quite clear. "Crants", sometimes printed "Grant" — a Scots Calvinist? — is here presumably some kind of European Calvinist, who therefore seeks the Church at Geneva, represented as a country wench:

plaine, simple, sullen, yong,
Contemptuous, yet unhansome. . .

As lecherous men, men who have some strange tastes, choose coarse country drudges:

Graius stayes still at home here, and because
Some preachers, vile ambitious bauds, and lawes
Still new like fashions, bid him thinke that shee
Which dwels with us, is onely perfect, hee
Imbraceth her,

So that even the Church of England is not right simply because it happens to be on the spot. Then he deals with other varieties. "Phrygius" says that they're all wrong, just as because some women are whores he won't trust women. "Gracchus" thinks they're really all the same thing. Both these views are wrong. Gracchus would be a sort of Neo-Platonist who thought of all religions as belonging to the same category; a kind of early Deist if you like. But that's bad — "this blind-/nesse to much light breeds"; You've got to choose, that's the point:

but unmoved thou
Of force must one, and forc'd but one allow;
And the right;

and he suggests, as everyone did at this time, that you do a little historical research, for what we are looking for, of course, is the true primitive Catholic Church; "aske thy father which is shee,/Let him aske his"; Heresy is almost as old as truth:

truth and falsehood bee
Neare twins, yet truth a little elder is;

This would explain a great deal of his reading in Divinity. Then he comes to a famous passage:

On a huge hill,
Cragged, and steep, Truth stands, and hee that will
Reach her, about must, and about must goe;

It's famous for the way in which the lines enact this going about, and the struggle uphill. And he goes on to insist that this struggle must be made; that it's not wrong to be doubtful, to enquire about the right way, but it is wrong to fall asleep while you're doing it. An active position of doubt is what is required.

The poem ends by saying that political pressures are not an excuse for making an untrue choice:

Keepe the truth which thou'hast found; men do not stand
In so'ill case here, that God hath with his hand
Sign'd Kings blanck-charters to kill whome they hate,
Nor are the Vicars, but hangmen to Fate.

"Blanck-charters" were things that Richard II made noblemen sign. They were really blank cheques. The nobleman signed and he filled in the figure. What he says here is that God has not given kings absolute permission to fill in whatever name they choose on blank death-warrants. If they do that they are not the representatives of Fate but her executioners, hangmen.

Foole and wretch, wilt thou let thy Soule be ty'd
To mans lawes, by which she shall not be try'd

At the last day?

Are you going to pay attention to the law of the land and not the Law of Heaven which will judge your Fate for eternity?

Will it then boot thee
To say a Philip, or a Gregory,
A Harry, or a Martin taught thee this?

A Philip of Spain, a Pope Gregory, Henry VIII and Martin Luther. Henry VIII was responsible, of course, for the foundation of the Church of England.

Is not this excuse for mere contraries,
Equally strong? Cannot both sides say so?

This doesn't get at the truth. Anybody can say I had to do that, because that's the way the law of the land was. There was a doctrine that people would have liked to impose at the time which said that a person's religion should be the religion of his region. They didn't want everybody involved in these religious controversies, so you should take the religion of your king. This is what is being contested here; you must not obey power when it becomes tyranny. That is where the poem ends.

Well you can see how important that poem is and how very vivid — one of the few privileged looks at Donne that we get — the young Donne in the 1590's with this tremendous pressure on him, and a lot of this pressure gets into the important *Third Satyre*. The other *Satyres*, as I've said, are less extraordinary. This one is a very unusual and exceptional poem.

VI

DONNE: LECTURE FOUR

FRANK KERMODE

In this lecture I want to talk to you about the poetry written after Donne's marriage, excluding any Songs and Sonnets that may have been written in the first decade of the seventeenth century. What we are left with is a great batch of occasional verse written, you will remember, at a bad time in Donne's life, when his marriage had ruined his worldly career and he simply had to write a lot of this poetry for patrons. Anyway, there they are, a great batch of funeral elegies, epithalamia and verse letters. Not all of them written for gain; some were written to friends.

You'll hardly, I think, want to familiarize yourself with every single line of every one of these verse letters. They have many of the characteristics that we have learned to recognise, for example, a kind of witty and contorted argument, but a great many of them are lacking in any kind of sensuous attractiveness and it would be wrong to pretend that if only these survived of Donne's works anyone would treat him as a major poet. But you can see who wrote them all right from the consistent use of theological and scientific themes for the purposes of an argument; of false argument, of course.

Take, to give an instance, the letter to the Countess of Bedford beginning "Reason is our Soules left hand." The Countess of Bedford was very important to Donne from about 1608, which is presumably the date of this poem, because at this stage, as you can tell, he didn't know her intimately. I will make one or two remarks on the poem just to key it into the poetry you already know:

Madame,
Reason is our Soules left hand, Faith her right,
By these wee reach divinity, that's you;
Their loves, who have the blessings of your light,
Grew from their reason, mine from faire faith grew.

But as, although a squint lefthandednesse
Be'ungracious, yet we cannot want that hand,
So would I, not to encrease, but to expresse
My faith, as I beleeve, so understand.

Therefore I study you first in your Saints,
Those friends, whom your election glorifies,
Then in your deeds, accesses, and restraints,
And what you reade, and what your selfe devize.

But soone, the reasons why you'are lov'd by all,
Grow infinite, and so passe reasons reach,
Then back againe to'implicite faith I fall,
And rest on what the Catholique voice doth teach.

There's no need to go on with it. You can see that it's gross piece of flattery, but couched in theological terms. Notice the stanzas beginning, as usual, with a switch — "But," "Therefore," "But" and so on. There's this method of argument and the argument is based on the theological proposition that faith and reason are both ways of access to the Divine Truth, which he identifies with the Countess of Bedford. He places them: faith on the right hand, reason on the left. Other people know her well and therefore don't have to use faith, which is, of course a confidence in things unseen. He wants, however, to know her so that his reason can support his faith and he studies her in her saints — people whom she has elected as God elects His saints, namely her friends. But soon he says, the reason side looms too large. It becomes altogether too patently obvious why she is loved and why she is goodness itself, and so he falls back on faith. It's all very trivial, really, but it's a trivial use of a quite solid theological argument.

Some of the letters are deliberately made obscure, as a kind of joke. There's the letter to Sir Edward Herbert beginning "Man is a lumpe," which I'm not going to discuss but which is a good example of this. Edward Herbert was a very good poet, incidentally, in some of his work as good a poet as Donne. They were friends from early times and clearly did have competitions in obscurity. In fact, as Jonson said of Donne, he wrote the *Elegy on the Death of Prince Henry* "to match Sir Edward Herbert in obscureness," and this is one of his most difficult and also one of his worst poems. There's a good deal of this kind of thing.

Another element in the Verse Letters which it's worth looking out for is an occasional reference to something that's interesting in the autobiography of the poet, relevant, perhaps, to his giving up poetry. His reference to his own style — "I sing not, Siren like, to tempt; for I/Am harsh" comes from a verse letter.[1]

Another verse letter is the one *To Mr. B.B.* — "Is not thy sacred hunger of science/Yet satisfy'd?" — which has an interesting conclusion, explaining in a rather feeble passage — perhaps appropriately feeble — why he can no longer write really good poetry:

My muse, (for I had one), because I'am cold,
    Divorc'd her selfe: the cause being in me,
    That I can take no new in Bigamye,
Not my will only but power doth withhold.
Hence comes it, that these Rymes which never had
    Mother, want matter, and they only have
    A little forme, the which their Father gave;
They are prophane, imperfect, oh, too bad
    To be counted Children of Poetry
    Except confirmed and Bishoped by thee.

Now that is characteristic of bad seventeenth-century witty writing. However, it has this special interest: what he's saying is, I gave up the Muse and can't marry another one, not only because I don't want to but because I'm forbidden to — presumably referring to his new ecclesiastical responsibilities. "Hence comes it, that these Rymes which never had/Mother, want matter."

This is an idea which you had better know about because it crops up again in Renaissance poetry. It is simply that the mother provides a sort of matrix, which is matter, and the father provides the form. It's a rather crude embryology. Man simply imposes his form on the chaotic material in the woman from which the child is born; this notion was reinforced by a quite false etymology which related the Latin word for mother with the Latin word for matter — *mater* and *materia*. (You'll find this is important when you read Spenser. This whole idea of the male providing the form and the female providing the matter is essential to one of Spenser's central episodes, The Garden of Adonis.)[2] What Donne is

---

1. *To Mr. S. B.*
2. *F.Q.* III. *vi.*

saying here is that he has nothing to write about now, so his poems lack mother or matter. What they have is a little form which their father gave them. Then he treats them as children who are unregenerate and whom his friend can, as it were, save by confirming them into the Church.

Well, I think that that's a brief but perhaps useful glimpse at the sort of thing that goes on in the Verse Letters. I'll say no more about them but will get on to the principal works of this period, and the longest and in many ways the most ambitious poems that Donne ever wrote, namely the two *Anniversaries.*

These are about, or the occasion of them is, the death of a young girl, Elizabeth Drury, who died just before she was fifteen. She was the daughter of a rich friend and patron of Donne, the man after whom Drury Lane was named, and at one time he lent Donne a house there. When Elizabeth Drury died — curiously it seems that Donne never met her — he did what was quite normal at the time and presented her father with a funeral elegy. That's the one that comes at the end of the first *Anniversary.* That was in 1609. He then had the idea of a rather more elaborate affair. The whole account of how it came about you can read in Ball's biography.

Having written the first *Anniversary,* Donne actually did go with Drury to France and he spent the winter there. The *Anatomy of the World* was published in 1611 and the second *Anniversary, of The Progress of the Soule*, which was written during the time in France, was published in the following year. There seemed to be some idea that Donne would go on writing an annual poem in memory of Elizabeth Drury, but, for whatever reason, this was not done, perhaps because he took orders in 1614 and gave up writing poetry practically altogether.

Anyway, only two *Anniversaries* exist and I suppose that, on the whole, people are not altogether displeased by that. Even at the time these poems seem to have incurred a certain amount of hostile criticism, crystallized for us in Ben Jonson's remark that they were "prophane and full of blasphemies." Jonson was an ex-Catholic and thought that it was quite wrong to talk about a human being as Donne talks about Elizabeth Drury. He said that "if it had been written of the Virgin Mary it would have been something," and he reports Donne's reply, which was that he was describing the idea of a woman and not an individual.

Donne makes another defence in a letter, in which he says that naturally if you are doing a funeral elegy on somebody you do the best you can. The whole purpose of such an elegy is to put the person in the best possible light and one of the ways you can do that is by saying that now she is dead the whole world is like a carcass and a ruin. However, I'm not sure about the defence he made to Jonson — "the idea of a woman and not as she was." It seems to me that a more convincing defence can be got from the titles of the poems, the first of which is *An Anatomy of the World. Wherein, by occasion of the Untimely Death of Mistress Elizabeth Drury, the frailty and the Decay of this Whole World is Represented.* Well, "by occasion of," that's all right isn't it? He uses the death of this girl to meditate upon the frailty and decay of the whole world; and similarly in *The Progresse of the Soul. Wherein, by Occasion of the Religious Death of Mistress Elizabeth Drury the Incommodities of the Soule in this life, and her Exaltation in the Next, are Contemplated* — again, the use of occasion.

Now these poems employ two very common themes in Renaissance poetry and in a characteristic way. You get the progress of the soul and you get lamentations about the decay of the world, very frequently. I'll say a little more about that in a minute. But you don't get them in this curiously witty form. Donne is here trying to solve a problem which must often have occurred to him, namely how to write a long poem in a manner which is really highly appropriate for short poems: to propel a very long, structured poem by these squibs and conceits. It is as if the motive power of the poem were little jokes and conceits, quite serious jokes; the kind of jokes people sometimes put in sermons and which are sometimes called "jokes for God's sake." But to keep up that prolonged and morbidly conceited, witty writing through a long poem and still give the poem a structure was really quite a large technical challenge; to combine "strong lines," if you like, with an articulated structure of this length. So that makes them, I think, worth looking at.

In the first *Anniversary, An Anatomie*, "anatomie" means what we should call a dissection: the cutting up of a corpse. And that's what he's doing. He's cutting up the corpse of the world, supposing that it's a corpse, because its soul, namely Elizabeth Drury, has disappeared from it. It's the same notion as that you get in the short poem, *A Feaver*, in the *Songs and Sonnets*, and in other poems of the same kind. He's making the woman the soul of the world.

The soul of the world is another idea that you get very often in Renaissance poetry; it's ultimately a platonic idea. The idea is that the world is infused (it crops up again in a very different form in Wordsworth) with a sort of divine force that enables things to grow and generate. This is a reflection of the creative force of God, and if you remove this *anima mundi* then what you've got left is simply a dead thing. He's also got in mind the myth about the goddess Astraea — we'll be hearing a lot more about her, too, when we come to Spenser. She was the last to leave the Earth at the end of the Golden Age and her departure was the signal for decline in the creation, which, if you look at it that way, has been going on ever since. She was the Goddess of Justice.

The idea of the decay of the world, upon which this first poem depends, is again one that deserves a certain amount of consideration. It is a very, very common idea in the poetry of the period and in the sermons of the period. It may seem strange as a feature of Renaissance poetry, "Renaissance" meaning rebirth, that one of most constant themes is death, the decline and death and decay of the world. This is so common that a famous book written in 1630 by a man called Hakewill begins with a protest at what he says is the general belief — that the world is in decay. You get this in Donne encapsulated in the famous phrase "Tis all in pieces, all coherence gone." That is the title of a book on the subject by Victor Harris, *All Coherence Gone*, which fully documents this *fin de siècle* notion — because one identifies it with the period about 1600 — that the world is in decay. It's another thing that crops up in a curious form at the end of the nineteenth century when, as Oscar Wilde said, it was not only "*fin de siècle*" but "*fin du globe*." It happens at the end of both these centuries, and others too. Anyway, it was very strong at the end of the sixteenth and the beginning of the seventeenth centuries and the so-called Jacobean melancholy of which you get so much in the drama of the period is, in a way, an aspect of this.

In using this theme Donne is not inventing a new style of morbidity; everybody thought that this was the worst age of the world, at least in some moods they thought this:

As the world grows in years 'tis heavens curse,

Mens sins increase, the pristine times were best;

The ages in their growth wax worse and worse.

Behind this, once again, there's a classical myth: the descent from Gold and Silver right down to our own Iron age. And of course this existed, as ideas always do, concurrently with a different set of ideas, namely the notion of — as Bacon put it — the antiquity of time and the youth of the world: *antiquitas seculi, iuventus mundi.* We are actually grown up and the ancients were as children in regard to us, so that we can do things better than they can; not because they are inferior beings but as if they were giants and we dwarfs, so that if you put the dwarf on the giant's shoulders it can see further.

This was a well-known figure at the time and it is quite an interesting little emblem of how the Renaissance saw itself. It is important for the idea of progress, which became a central seventeenth-century concept. The switch into what was called modern and the devaluation of ancient models somewhat depended on this notion that even if we are smaller people, we can see further. You get these disparate ideas quite openly co-existing in the same mind, and as we are able to see it, so it presumably will be easy for people to see it in us in three hundred years time — that we act on the basis of all sorts of mutually contradictory doctrines.

Anyway, Donne in this poem (and I think temperamentally), favoured the idea of the world being, as it were, on its last legs. This includes, of course, recent evidence that things were not right in the heavens. I don't mean simply Copernicus. I think that is nearly always rather overplayed when people are talking about Donne. It's not really as upsetting as all that to be told that we are going round the sun instead of vice versa, because it doesn't make that much difference to people. What *is* upsetting is the appearance in heaven of a new star — a nova — and there were several of these and some very brilliant ones. I'm no astronomer and I can't tell you about them, but in the 1570's and after, people were very upset by these phenomena because they thought that the heavens were incorruptible; everything above the moon was supposed to be incorruptible and, therefore, could not generate.

So the appearance of a new star was quite an upsetting event. The evidence is that people were much more distressed by that than they were by Copernicus. This will apply not only to Donne, but, as you will see, in the Vth Book of the *F.Q.*, to Spenser. It was a common enough worry that the heavens were going awry in one way or another; the planets didn't seem to be keeping to their courses, were showing up late, and that kind of thing. It is partly improved observation that made these discoveries, and observations of apparent irregularities, possible. We are still a few years short of the discovery that planets do not move in circular orbits and until the elliptical orbit was understood, people were bound to get all this wrong, as indeed they did. Anyway, it could be used as evidence that mutability, as Spenser called it — change, decay — was rife, not only on Earth and among human beings but also in the heavens themselves. This view was quite congenial to Donne, especially in his more meditative moments.

By the time he wrote these poems (1615), he was already a convinced Anglican with years and years of theological study behind him and a great deal of writing in the field of religious controversy, theology and casuistry: the study of suicide (*Biathanatos*), the attack on Jesuits, the *Pseudo-Martyr*, and the *Essays in Divinity*. In fact, he was a highly practised and habitual theologian. The argument about when he became a convinced Anglican, as distinct from one who found it convenient to be an Anglican, is a long one and I don't know that it matters very much. Certainly it seems rather improper to say that he didn't really get converted until his wife died in 1617, when he had already been ordained three years. I think we must take it that these poems do reflect a very serious set of religious convictions, though of course they extend them in a rather melodramatic way.

Both the poems have traditional religious themes. The first of them is a very ancient one, namely the contempt of the world, *contemptus mundi*. People were very keen on death at this time. They liked death's-heads and you may know what a histrionic death-bed scene Donne had — having himself covered in a winding sheet while he was actually dying. So the *contemptus mundi* was rather a congenial theme; people liked the morbidity of it. The theme of the second poem is, as I've said, the mystical ascent of the soul.

There's one more thing to say about them by way of introduction and that is that probably, to put it no more strongly, they are designed according to a system of meditation which is, as it were, prefabricated. There are five meditations in the first poem and seven in the second. These formal meditations also affect the design of the *Holy Sonnets*. There have always been, of course, techniques of meditation, but the one that scored a great success in the sixteenth century was devised by St. Ignatius Loyola, the founder of the Jesuit order. It was used a great deal in various Jesuit-controlled sodalities; so you might think it would be banished in the reformed churches, but it was not. People knew a good thing when they saw it. They lost the use of the rosary, which you could call a piece of meditative technology; that had gone, but they rather liked this one instead. I won't go into details of it now, except in one respect, and this, I think, does come out in the *Anniversaries*.

The first part of the act of meditation was what St. Ignatius called a *composition of place.* You can read all about this in Martz's book *The Poetry of Meditation.* I ought to tell you that not everybody agrees with it, but you can make up your own mind about it. I think that it's right in a general way, if not in detail. The composition of place, or *compositio loci,* is the point where you try to enlist all of your senses as well as your mind in the contemplation of some imagined scene of religious significance. It might be the crucifixion, it might be your death bed, it might be the last day, the Judgement Day, it might be anything. Then you must enlist all the powers of your soul, not just the intellectual powers, and try to feel it − not just think about it, but try to feel it with your entire psychic organization. That's the first stage of the meditation. I will not go into the others at the moment, but in these *Anniversaries* you can occasionally see that the opening of a section is something that is quite reasonable to describe as a composition of place.

In the first of the *Anniversaries,* each of the five sections has three parts. First a meditation, founded on some theme such as I have mentioned; then a eulogy of Elizabeth Drury; and then a refrain and a moral, saying what comes out of this and how corrupt the world is in relation to her pure soul. The second Anniversary, except for the very first section, drops the refrain.

The first part of the first *Anniversary,* "To the Praise of the Dead," is not by Donne at all; it is by Joseph Hall. Donne begins with what he calls the "entrie into the worke." The first section, the first ninety lines, are a general introduction on the idea of the world as dead and putrified:

Sicke world, yea, dead, yea putrified, since shee
Thy'intrinsique balme, and thy preservative,

Can never be renew'd, thou never live,
I (since no man can make thee live) will try,
What wee may gaine by thy Anatomy.

(56-60)

— that's to say, by cutting you up, by dissecting you. And then we go on from
that to the first section which is about the decay of man, "Impossibility of
health." This starts at line 91:

There is no health; Physitians say that wee,
At best, enjoy but a neutralitie.
And can there bee worse sicknesse, than to know
That we are never well, nor can be so?
Wee are borne ruinous: poore mothers cry,
That children come not right , nor orderly;
Except they headlong come and fall upon
An ominous precipitation.
How witty's ruine!

(91-99)

That's totally characteristic of the tone of these poems. They're serious and
gloomy and yet they contain a number of very absurd conceits like that one of
children being born upside down. And then he goes on, in the course of this first
section, to speak about the shortness of human life now in relation to human life
in the past. This is another favourite theme of the period. This is partly based on
the Book of Genesis, where everybody seems to be at least eight hundred years
old and some people live to be nine hundred years old. The general feeling was
not that the expression "year" had altered its meaning, but that life had grown a
great deal shorter. Donne dwells on that with his usual sort of hyperbole and
witty extensions of the idea:

who lives to age,
Fit to be made *Methusalem* his page?
Alas, we scarce live long enough to try
Whether a true made clocke run right, or lie.

(127-130)

This is typical hyperbole, if you like. We don't even live long enough to find
out whether our watches are running fast or slow. And of course the mention of
Methusalah reinforces that. And this decline affects our size, too:

mankinde decayes so soone,
We'are scarce our Fathers shadows cast at noone:

(143-4)

At noon we have no shadow at all, really, and that's our size in relation to our Father's. The notion that people are getting smaller and smaller has died now, because people are obviously getting bigger and bigger; but it's a long standing notion that you get in all kinds of folk tales. We've not given up the idea that in an heroic past every one was very much larger, lived longer and ate more. Donne has to relate all this to the death of Elizabeth Drury, which he does in the eulogy which begins at line 175:

Shee, of whom th'Ancients seem'd to prophesie,
When they call'd vertues by the name of *shee*;
Shee in whom vertue was so much refin'd,
That for Allay unto so pure a minde
Shee tooke the weaker Sex;

(175-179)

That's interesting because he explains why this paragon of all things should be a woman, and that is because she was so incredibly virtuous that, as with pure gold, you had to put a baser metal in her to make her useful; therefore it would be better to take a woman's body than a man's as being somewhat baser than a man's.

shee that could drive
The poysonous tincture, and the staine of *Eve,*
Out of her thoughts, and deeds; and purifie
All, by a true religious Alchymie;

(179-182)

Note that idea of the true alchemy against the implicit false one that we had in the *Nocturnall.* Then the refrain:

Shee, shee is dead; shee's dead: when thou knowest this,
Thou knowest how poore a trifling thing man is.

That's the end of the first section. The second section, as the marginal note says, is about the "Decay of nature in other parts." Men in their world are lame. The angels fell and therefore men will fall. That's another popular theme of meditation, incidentally. And then finally again, the eulogy and the refrain:

Shee, shee is dead; shee's dead: when thou knowest this,
Thou knowest how lame a cripple this world is.

(237-8)

The third meditation begins at line 247. It is called "Disformity of parts," that is to say, how disproportion has got into the world and not only into the world, but into the sky. And he talks again, not about new astronomy but about the solar ecliptic and so on. He's not really saying that things have recently gone bad, he is saying that they have always been so. This is a bit like the Proem in the Vth Book of the *Faerie Queene*

So, of the Starres which boast that they do runne
In Circle still, none ends where he began. . .

(275-6)

It looks as though there's some disorder in the heavens as well as on the earth. Then there's a complaint that the Earth is anything but perfect, because if it were so it would be smooth and circular; but it has, in fact, very high hills, like the one at "Tenarif":

Doth not a Tenarif, or higher Hill
Rise so high like a Rocke, that one might thinke
The floating moone would shipwrack there, and sinke?

(286-88)

The world has lost proportion, it's thoroughly mis-shapen, whereas she — and we get to the eulogy, line 309 — she has all proportion, all symmetry, all harmony and now she's left us. And again the refrain:

Shee, shee is dead, shee's dead; when though knowest this,
Thou knowest how ugly a monster this world is.

(325-6)

Section four, beginning at 338, is about the loss of colour and lustre from the world. It takes the same kind of form, the eulogy follows, and the refrain at line 369. The fifth section is about how our connections with heaven are no longer as strong as they used to be; these are influences of stars, not only on people but on all growing things. This has passed. Her departure is another measure of how much we've lost in this respect also.

And so we go on to the sixth section and the funeral elegy, but I don't think it's necessary to go into it in any more detail. You can see what sort of thing it is and you can see that having written it and gained a certain confidence he was ready to do something even more elaborate — which he did in the *Second Anniversary, The Progresse of the Soule.*

"The Harbinger; of the Progresse" we shall ignore, and begin at "The Entrance." Now this is a much more clearly articulated poem than the other one and it is also more difficult and more fantastic. It's much more important, I think, for a general knowledge of Donne. It's commonly thought of as the masterpiece among his longer poems and I agree with this. There are seven meditations in it and, as I say, the refrain is dropped at the end of the first meditation. He's dealing now with the plight of the imprisoned soul on Earth and, of course, he can have an "extasy," he can get outside the body as in the poem called *The Extasie.* This is another conventional theme — describing the ascent of the soul in ecstasy. You find it in another form in Milton's poem *At a Vacation Exercise,* for example. It considers how we on Earth deface God's image in us (another theme that Donne was very keen on), and considers Elizabeth Drury as a symbol of God's likeness in human form.

This poem seems to me to have a lot more economy than the other one and it's got some important things in it which I shall try to point out. The "entrance" is of course well known for that rather beautiful figure of the lute (line 19). "All these motions" which we have around us are not real motions at all, they're just involuntary motions as you might get in dead things. They

Are but as Ice, which crackles at a thaw:
Or as a Lute, which in moist weather, rings
Her knell alone, by cracking of her strings:
So struggles this dead world, now shee is gone;
For there is motion in corruption. . .

(18-22)

Then this notion of the corruption and decay of the world is spelled out in such lines as this, which comes from the first section, "A just disestimation of the world,"

The world is but a carkasse; thou art fed
By it, but as a worme, that carkasse bred. . .

(55-56)

The tone is very gloomy. Anyway, the first meditation begins at line 45 and the eulogy begins at line 65 and then there's the refrain at line 81:

Shee, shee is gone; shee is gone; when thou knowest this
What fragmentary rubbidge this world is
Thou knowest, and that it is not worth a thought;

We then come to a really authentic composition of place which is called in the margin "Contemplation of our state in our death-bed" – a very common recurring theme for meditation. (Contemplation and meditation mean much the same thing for writers at the time.) This is a very famous passage:

Thinke then, my soule, that death is but a Groome,
Which brings a Taper to the outward roome,
Whence thou spiest first a little glimmering light,
And after brings it nearer to the sight:
For such approaches doth heaven make in death.
Thinke thy selfe labouring now with broken breath,
And think those broken and soft Notes to bee
Division, and thy happiest Harmonie.

(85-92)

Thinke thee laid on thy death-bed, loose and slacke
And thinke that, but unbinding of a packe,

> To take one precious thing, thy soule from thence.
>
> (93-95)

"Division" is a technical name for playing variations on a musical theme. Again there is a series of quite unrelated hyperbolical figures by which he enforces, with some intensity, this notion of being on one's death-bed. Then in the third section, beginning line 157, he goes on to say that the Soul is bound to two lower souls. This is a traditional idea; the vegetative soul, which is responsible for growth, and the sensible soul, which is responsible for movement, and the rational soul, which is responsible for choice. That particular distinction goes back as far as Aristotle. The rational soul, the higher soul, is bound to need two lower souls and inhabits, as it was generated in, filth. This is medieval stuff; you can take it back to the Church Fathers. It's a "disestimation," if you like, of the body, it's a way of saying that the human body is rather a disgusting object.

> Thinke, when 'twas growne to most, 'twas a poore Inne,
>
> A province pack'd up in two yards of skinne,
>
> (175-6)

That makes him six feet high, incidentally, which, considering men were getting smaller, is not bad. Then there's an extraordinary figure, which is very like Donne at his most extravagant, of the bullet which, when it's fired, blows up the gun.

> Thinke that a rustie Peece, discharg'd, is flowne
>
> In peeces, and the bullet is his owne,
>
> And freely flies:
>
> (181-3)

The bullet is the soul and the rusty old gun is the body which falls apart. There's a good deal of that kind of excessive figuration in these poems and very often he does keep it going pretty steadily for long stretches.

The ascent of the soul begins at line 187, describing the ascent of Elizabeth Drury' soul. As I say, it's compared to a gas, to a bullet, to a new-born chicken, all within six lines. At line 220 the eulogy begins; she, of course, is not imprisoned in the body; and so on. We come to a very famous passage here about which I must briefly say a word because it is so often quoted:

> She, of whose soule, if we may say, 'twas Gold,
>
> Her body was th'Electrum, and did hold
>
> Many degrees of that; wee understood
>
> Her by her sight; her pure and eloquent blood
>
> Spoke in her cheekes, and so distinctly wrought,
>
> That one might almost say, her body thought.
>
> (241-6)

This is sometimes applied to a supposed union of sense and wit — sensualness and wit — if you like, in Donne's own poetry — in fact it was so applied as early as the nineteenth century — "one might almost say, her body thought." You must understand the figure being used — it is again one of gold, being combined with silver. The proportion of silver in the gold entitled the resulting alloy to be called an "Electrum." The idea is that this kind of alloy has a peculiar glow, a brilliance that ordinary gold has not and it is as if the gold was glinting through the silver. That's the figure and it's a very elaborate one. You might say, in Coleridgean terms, that that's an act of imagination, whereas the one about the bullet is an act of fancy; there's a qualitative difference between the two.

There is, I am afraid, too little time to go over the rest in very much detail. You can pick out the sections beginning at line 321, the sixth at line 383 and the seventh at line 471. But one important passage I shall simply have to mention, and that's the one that begins at line 251 — about the ignorance of the soul in this life and in the next. This is a full treatment of the general idea of what is sometimes called scepticism. It is a very important religious idea; the notion that the human intellect is incapable of achieving any kind of truth about any matter that is of importance at all. Now Donne develops this at great length:

> Have not all soules though
> For many ages, that our body 'is wrought
> Of Ayre, and Fire, and other Elements?

(263-5)

And then along come people and say it isn't. And now, he says, what do we know? We don't know very much. We don't know how we get bladder stones for examples, we don't know how the blood circulates; and so on through a long list. If we don't know these little things how are we ever going to know the really big things?

> We see in Authors, too stiffe to recant,
> A hundred controversies of an Ant;
> And yet one watches, starves, freeses, and sweats,
> To know but Catechismes and Alphabets
> Of unconcerning things, matters of fact;

(281-5)

That's a line worth remembering — "unconcerning things, matters of fact." Matters of fact were for Donne relatively unimportant. The only things of any real concern to the human being were divine truths. It's a very old idea this — that any knowledge which doesn't actually promote the salvation of your soul is really at best indifferent and, at worst, harmful.

> How others on our stage their parts did Act;
> What *Caesar* did, yea, and what *Cicero* said.

Why grasse is greene, or why our blood is red,
Are mysteries which none have reach'd unto.
In this low forme, poore soule, what wilt thou doe?
When wilt thou shake off this Pedantery,
Of being taught by sense, and Fantasie?
Thou look'st through spectacles; small things seem great
Below; But up unto the watch-towre get,
And see all things desployl'd of fallacies:
Thou shalt not peepe through lattices of eyes,
Nor heare through Labyrinths of eares, nor learne
By circuit, or collections to discerne.
In heaven thou straight know'st all, concerning it,
And what concernes it not; shalt straight forget.

(286-300)

"Fantasie" here means imagination, a lower function of the mind. This is very simple and emphatic, a well-executed expression of something that went very deep in Donne, I think — this sceptical feeling. In his love poetry, it makes him tend to a certain libertinism, because the conventions and laws which control sexual behaviour seem absurd, man-made. In the same way, when you take it at this level, all human knowledge has a certain irrelevance, except in so far as it's about the real Truth. The passage I haven't been able to talk about is the very famous one "And new Philosophy calls all in doubt" (*First Anniversary,* line 205). Notice it's "*And* new Philosophy" and not *the* new philosophy; it makes a difference. But you'll see if you look carefully that it's part of the same scepticism. Just as a lot of long-held opinions seem to him ridiculous and irrelevant to his serious concerns, so these new opinions are further evidence that the world is a bit of a mess and that we don't understand it.

Anyway, there's no doubt that these poems do run the risk of the censure that Donne himself passed, "when wee are mov'd to seeme religious/Only to vent wit, Lord deliver us." They've got far too much wit in them, so to speak, but there are some very fine things in them among all these frigidities. Sometimes you feel that they degenerate into a series of ingenious, morbid poetic wisecracks, but on the whole I think they do hold up. They are susceptible to the criticism of bad taste, which Jonson put forward, but I think that is a minor criticism. They are very interesting to us because they come in the middle of Donne's career, at the beginning of the end of it, in fact. They show him tackling, really for the first time, a very extensive poem — although it was an age of long poems — and doing it in what was materially a new way.

VII

DONNE: LECTURE FIVE

FRANK KERMODE

In this lecture I shall be talking almost entirely about Donne's religious work and I also want to say a few words about his prose.

Some time ago, when I was talking about the *Third Satyre*, I commented briefly on the early efforts Donne had made (and which are recorded, in a sense, in that *Satyre*) to choose between the religion into which he had been born — the Roman Catholic — and the state religion — the Anglican. Of course, as we know, he made the choice, for very good reasons — in so far as we know his reasons — for Anglicanism as we now call it.

Throughout his life, as he moved more and more into ecclesiastical and theological affairs — writing polemic against the Catholics and, finally, in 1614 becoming ordained — throughout that time, one thing is striking about his religious career and that is that he did not fall into a kind of rabid anti-Romanism, which was quite common during the period. He had very little time for Calvinists, indeed he thought their doctrines somewhat disgusting; the idea that God made us to damn us was a very disagreeable one to him. Nor did he have much time for the Jesuits, the most militant of the Roman Catholics. On the whole he kept the balance very well. You see this in the *Pseudo-Martyr*, which he wrote before his ordination. He attacks the Jesuits, as he had attacked them in *Ignatius his Conclave*, for their intolerance and their military posture. He says that the Churches must not despise one another, but should continue to hope to be reunited eventually.

One of the great events in sixteenth-century ecclesiastical history was the Council of Trent, which sat from the 1540's to the 1560's and which people thought at one time might be a way of bringing the Churches together again. But it turned out to be rather a divisive Council, and founded what we call the "Counter-Reformation," dividing the Churches yet more widely. Yet long after Trent and throughout Donne's lifetime there were people not only in England, but also in Italy and France, who saw some hope for at least tolerance between the Churches, what would be called an eirenic understanding between them, and some even hoped for union. Donne was very interested in all this and often preached about it.

He was quite clear in his own mind that he had chosen the right Church. He admired the English "middle way." This *via media* has a rather curious history. It had been enforced politically, and with great unpopularity, at the beginning of the reign of Elizabeth, and then justified the historical explanations given for it — as in the rewriting of Church history to make the Church of England seem the older of the two Churches, older than the Church of Rome. The great philosophical justification of the Church of England was given by Hooker in *The Laws of Ecclesiastical Polity,* a book which we shall come back to many times. These justifications were after the event, so to speak, but they were really none the worse for that. One of the things that happened — a real piece of luck in a way — was that having started her reign with a lot of corrupt and rather bad bishops, Elizabeth had the good fortune to find some clever ones, in fact some geniuses, later on. By the time Donne became the Dean of St. Paul's, there was a very powerful episcopal bench with some very notable figures and great preachers, like Lancelot Andrewes. Most connoisseurs of sermons will say that Andrewes was a greater preacher than Donne, although entirely different in style; much less openly emotional, much more learned in his manner. However, Donne in his own time was extremely famous as a preacher and I'll mention one or two of his sermons shortly.

After Donne's ordination he wrote very little poetry; even the *Holy Sonnets* were probably written between the 1590's and 1611, that is to say three years before he was ordained. But he did write at least three of the sonnets after that and a few occasional poems — the *Hymne to God my God, in my Sicknesse* and *A Hymne to God the Father,* and poems such as *Good Friday, 1613. Riding Westward,* and one or two others which I'll mention shortly. That is to say, he did not give up writing poetry altogether, but he ceased to think of himself as a poet. He often refers to his youth as the time of his poetry. He speaks slightingly of his earlier poems from time to time and it is notable that of the many elegies that were produced on his death in 1631, and printed by his son in 1633 in the first edition of his poems, very few have much to say about him as a poet. The notable exception, of course, is the elegy of Thomas Carew, a great poem,[1] and also one of the finest pieces of appreciative criticism of Donne there is. He does speak of Donne as a poet in the warmest and most suggestive terms; but others tended to refer to his poems as simply part of his youth; exploiting the over-simple Jack Donne/Dr. John Donne antithesis — the witty young man and the immensely sanctified parson. And that's the way he was thought of, and went on being thought of, for quite a while. In fact, even for someone like Coleridge, Donne was more famous as a divine than as a poet, although Coleridge, who read so much, also read the poems.

So, in all the period after 1614, in the seventeen remaining years of his life, we can't escape the fact that Donne is primarily a writer of prose and primarily a writer of sermons, although he did write other things as well.

Now Donne's prose is, as I say, an exceedingly large quantity of print. The sermons are in ten volumes, in one edition, and there are several quite substantial books — the *Essays in Divinity* and *Biathanatos* and so. (I don't really see how you can be expected to familiarize yourself with the entire extent of it.) There is a selection of prose, *John Donne: Selected Prose*, which is all right; anyway, it gives you an idea of the scope and leaves out a lot of the more boring books like *Pseudo-Martyr*. His early books like *Paradoxes and Problems* are worth looking at. These are pre-ordination, of course. The *Paradoxes* are very like some of the themes you get repeated in *Songs and Sonnets*, about woman's constancy and so on. You can see that many of the *Songs and Sonnets* are really verse paradoxes. *Ignatius his Conclave* is a sort of satire on the Jesuits and there are some fashionable references to Galileo and the telescope. *Biathanatos* is a casuistical exercise on suicide; on whether it's ever justified for a Christian. The *Essays in Divinity,* I'm told, are not highly regarded as theological exercises.

Leaving behind that early prose, we come now to the prose of the period following his ordination. One work in particular stands out apart from the Sermons, namely the *Devotions* which were published in 1623. They were written when Donne was seriously ill and thought he was dying.

Devotions is a very strange work. Each Devotion consists of three sections; a meditation, an expostulation, and a prayer, and in that respect they resemble the *Holy Sonnets* because they have a certain formality based on meditative traditions. But the theme of the meditation in each case is some developing aspect of his sickness; the doctor calls, for example, or they discuss the meaning

---

1. *An Elegie upon the death of the Deane of Pauls, Dr. John Donne.*

of certain rashes that appear on his body, and he meditates on these and expostulates about them and prays about them.

The most famous of these meditations, which clearly it would be remiss of me not to mention, is the one in which he hears the church bells tolling. This is more interesting than one might think merely from a little bit that's always quoted on its own. We'll look at the opening part of this, in fact the section from the meditation. The motto says "Now, this Bell tolling softly for another, saies to me, Thou must die."

Perchance hee for whom this *Bell* tolls, may be so ill, as that hee knowes not it tolls for him; And perchance I may thinke my selfe so much better than I am, as that they who are about mee, and see my state, may have caused it to toll for mee, and I know not that. The *Church* is *Catholike, universall,* so are all her *Actions; All* that she does, belongs to *all.* When she *baptizes a child,* that action concernes mee; for that child is thereby connected to that *Head* which is my *Head* too, and engrafed into that *body,* whereof I am a *member.* And when she *buries a Man,* that action concernes me: All *mankinde* is of one *Author,* and is one *volume;* when one Man dies, one *Chapter* is not *torne* out of the *booke,* but *translated* into a better *language;* and every *Chapter* must be so *translated; God* emploies several *translators;* some peeces are translated by *age,* some by *sicknesse,* some by *warre,* some by *justice;* but *Gods* hand is in every *translation;* and his hand shall binde up all our scattered leaves again, for his *Librarie* where every *booke* shall lie open to one another: As therefore the *Bell* that rings to a *Sermon,* calls not upon the *Preacher* only, but upon the *Congregation* to come; so this *Bell* calls us all: but how much more mee, who am brought so neere the *doore* by this *sicknesse.* There was a *contention* as farre as a *suite,* (in which both *pietie* and *dignitie, religion,* and *estimation,* were mingled) which of the religious *Orders* should ring to *praiers* first in the *Morning;* and it was *determined,* that *they should ring first that rose earliest.* If we understand aright the *dignitie* of this *Bell* that tolls for our *evening prayer,* we would bee glad to make it ours, by rising early, in that *application,* that it might bee ours, as well as his, whose indeed it is. The *Bell* doth toll for him that *thinkes* it doth; and though it *intermit* againe, yet from that *minute,* that that occasion wrought upon him, hee is united to *God.* Who casts not up his *Eye* to the *Sunne* when it rises? but who takes off his *Eye* from a *Comet* when that breakes out? Who bends not his *eare* to any *bell,* which is passing a *peece of himselfe* out of this *world?* No man is an *Iland,* intire of it selfe; every man is a peece of the *Continent,* a part of the maine; if a *Clod* bee washed away by the *Sea, Europe* is the lesse, as well as if a *Promontorie* were, as well as if a

Mannor of thy *friends* or of *thine owne* were; any mans *death* diminishes *me*, because I am involved in *Mankinde;* And therefore never send to know for whom the *Bell* tolls: It tolls for *thee.*

Now I read that out in the hope that you would follow the characteristic play, continuous from the early work, of figures. He doesn't stick constantly to the toll of the bell; the argument progresses by a series of images which start from the tolling of the bell but go into this elaborate figure of the book — God takes each one through the act of translation and the translators are called sickness, war, justice. Donne uses figures like that in a deadly serious argument and this simply confirms something we learn about Donne right at the beginning: that any kind of argument is propelled along by analogies of the kind that would be called witty. This is equally true in the secular prose as in the religious poetry, and it's worth remembering that, if one thinks that the mere fact of using that kind of argument implies a lack of seriousness. It doesn't. It implies a different attitude to analogies from any that we now commonly hold. If you read through this passage and listed the different sorts of figures, you'd see that the bell had not only that idea of the Bible in it but also the conceit of breaking off a piece of Europe, as well as several others.

Anyway, that's the way he begins the Devotion, and then he passes on to an expostulation, and a comment, and ends in a prayer. They belong to 1623 which is, incidentally, the same date as the *Hymne to God my God, in my Sickenesse,* which is another example of the same thing. It's a poem, by a man who presumably thinks that he is dying, which is so witty, so "far-fetched" according to old criticism, that many readers still have a lot of difficulty in understanding it; but I'll come back to that.

There are a great many sermons, as I've said; they are very long and they were extremely popular. Many of them were, of course, delivered at St. Paul's, some of them at St. Paul's Cross outside the Cathedral. You can dip into them anywhere. What you do find, listening to them being read, is that you do have to concentrate because so much is happening. The line of the argument bends and twists. Donne always stays with his text; it's really all quite systematic. But within that system, the false leads, the sudden bends in one direction or another, are really of a sort that means the listener — and an hour and a half was presumably the length of most of these sermons — has really got to be on duty for the whole time.

This is worth remembering when we think of one characteristic of Donne's age which is so obvious that we tend to ignore it, and that is that people must have been very good at listening. If you could follow a sermon of Donne's then you could go to the Globe Theatre and make sense of, say, *Coriolanus.* Obviously people did go to the Globe Theatre and make out what *Coriolanus* was about, although we find it quite difficult to do so. It's difficult to imagine people following some of the later verse of Shakespeare at first hearing and yet Shakespeare was very much a man of business and knew his audience. His audience was in some measure the same audience as would go to St. Paul's Cross to hear Dr. Donne and they would use the same faculties; these being, to be quite simple about it, much more highly developed in the region of oral performance, whereas ours are much more highly developed on the printed page than theirs were.

Here's a bit from a sermon which will give you some idea if you haven't one already. It is a sermon of 1619, rather a famous one, which was preached just before he went off to Germany on a sort of mission. It has, as his sermons occasionally have, a slight personal flavour. (There is another sermon in which he speaks of the death of his daughter.) Here he does speak of his departure to Germany, but he's keeping more to his text, which is "Remember now thy Creator in the days of thy youth." I take this part because there is no doubt that the general tone of Donne's sermons is extremely gloomy, sometimes spectacularly so, as in the famous last sermon, *Death's Duel.* But he often does meditate in that way on corruption, decay, sin and death, which is the great theme, in some ways, of the sermons — how you die. There are some memorable figures using St. Paul's churchyard, for example — the idea that even if the dust gets into your eyes you should consider that it may be your father who's incommoding you at that point. This is a fairly characteristic lamentation, or rather not a lamentation so much as a serious injunction to his audience to heed the text — "Remember now thy Creator in the days of thy youth"; the comparison between the powers of youth and the impotence of old age. You will notice the characteristic mingling of homely English, rather grand English, and lots of Latin. This is because Donne tended to quote from the Vulgate translation of the Bible rather than the King James version, though this was available by the time he was preaching.

> Wouldest thou consecrate a Chalice to God that is broken? no man would present a lame horse, a disordered clock, a torn book to the king. *Caro jumentum,* thy body is thy beast; and wilt thou present that to God, when it is lam'd and tir'd with excesse of wantonnes? when thy clock (the whole course of thy time) is disordered with passions, and perturbations; when thy book (the history of thy life) is torn, one thousand sins of thine own torn out of thy memory, wilt thou present thy self thus defac'd and mangled to almighty God?

Notice that even in a sermon once he gets this idea going — of a lame horse, a disordered clock and a torn book – he uses the figures again to press the point; you can't offer an inadequate sacrifice to God.

Temperantia non est temperentia in senectute, sed impotentia incontinentiae, chastity is not chastity in old age, but a disability to be unchaste.

There again, you've got a Latin proverb and a very lively English translation:

And therefore thou dost not give God that which thou pretendest to give, for thou has no chasitity to give him. *Senex bis puer* (an old man is twice a child), but it is not *bis juvenis* (twice a youth); an old man comes to the infirmities of childhood again; but he comes not to the strength of youth again.

Do this then *In diebus juvenis,* in thy best strength, and when thy natural faculties are best able to concur with grace; but do it *In diebus electionum,* in the dayes when thou hast thy hearts desire; for if thou have worn out this word, in one sense, that it be too late now *to remember him in the dayes of youth,* (that's spent forgetfully) yet as long as thou art able to make a new choise, to chuse a new sin, that when thy heats of youth are not overcome, but burnt out, then thy middle age chooses ambition, and thy old age choose covetousness; as long as thou art able to make thy choice thou art able to make a better than this; God testifies that power, that he hath given thee; *I call heaven and earth to record this day that I have set before you life and death? choose life:* If this choice like you not, *if it seem evil unto you to serve the Lord,* saith *Josua,* then *choose ye this day whom you will serve.* Here's the election day; bring that which ye would have into comparison with that which you should have; that is; all that this world keeps from you, with that which God offers to you; and what will ye choose to prefer before him? For honor, and favor, and health, and riches, perchance you cannot have them though you choose them; but can you have more of them than they had, to whom those very things have been occasions of ruin? The Market is open till the bell ring; till the last bell ring the Church is open, grace is to be had there: but trust not upon that rule, that men buy cheapest at the end of the market, that heaven may be had for a breath at last, when they that hear it cannot tell whether it be a sigh or a gasp, a religious breathing and anhelation after the next life, or natural breathing out and exhalation of this; but find a spiritual good husbandry in that other rule, that the prime of the market is to be had at first: for howsoever, in thine age, there may be by Gods strong working, *Dies juventutis,* A day of youth, in making thee then a new creature; (for so God is *Antiquissimus dierum,* so in his school no man is superannuated) yet when age has made a man impotent to sin this is not *Dies electionum,* it is not a day of choice; but remember God now, when thou has a choice, that is, a power to advance thy self, or to oppress others by evil means; now in *die electionum,* in these thy happy and sunshine dayes, *remember him.*

Most of this is in one sentence and that again is very characteristic of Donne. You'll notice the drop into the homely figure — very characteristic also of his friend George Herbert — with the bell that says the market is closing and asking whether it is wiser to arrive there early and get the best. This elaborate comparison between the market and the church is just as typical as the air of learning which is generated as he goes along. The working in of many scriptural texts is part of the technique, but he's always sticking to the basic text — "Remember now thy Creator in the days of thy youth" — and quoting it in Latin from time to time.

There's much more that one could go on to say about this; for example, the comparison between the breaths. Don't leave it till the last minute, he says, when what you take to be a breath of last-minute repentance, a breath of new life, is mistaken by other people for just the end of this one; a breathing in of the next life — an "anhelation," or just a breathing out of this one — an "exhalation." This combination of English and Latin words — exhalation and anhelation — may remind you of other prose of the time, for example Shakespeare's, and not only of prose but verse. *Hamlet* is absolutely alive with these "doublets," I suppose you could call them, of Latin and English words. It's a way of satisfying learning and still letting people know what you're talking about, though certainly in Shakespeare it is rather more than that. It's a way of actually qualifying the sense.

But we mustn't get into *Hamlet* now. This is a characteristic of the time and again you must think of this as an oral performance that was not altogether unrelated to the kind of thing that was going on just across the river in Southwark, at the theatre, at the very time as he preached. Now I must say something about the holy poems.

Perhaps I should say, as first priority, that I don't myself set a great deal of store by these poems. They seem to me that on any unprejudiced view — or perhaps it is a prejudiced view — to be greatly inferior to the secular poetry, but that's not an opinion that I want in any way to enforce on anybody; it's clearly something about which one has to make up one's mind. I won't say anything about the the *Corona* sequence, the linked sonnets which are really meant to be a sort of rosary and which, in my view, are not very interesting. The most important of the holy poems, of course, are the *Holy Sonnets.* All these sonnets, except for three, belong to the period 1609-1611. The three later ones are about the death of his wife in 1617, the defeat of the Protestants at the Battle of the

White Mountain — the defeat of the Elector of Bohemia, who was of course the son-in-law of James I, in 1620 — and one other which is almost definitely of later date. Now that leaves sixteen, and four of those are additional to two sequences of six which appeared in the first edition of 1633. The order in which they appeared in 1633 is the correct order. For various reasons this was thought to be incorrect for a long time, but the order has now been restored by Helen Gardner in her edition of the *Divine Poems*, which was published a few years ago, and there is no point in adopting Grierson's sequence and his numbers. However, some of you may have texts in which they are wrongly numbered and I will point this out as we go along.

This wouldn't matter were it not now clear that these sonnets are in two sets of six and each set represents a coherent sequence. The first six, which in the Grierson numbering are 2, 4, 6, 7, 9 and 10 (in the Gardner edition, of course, they are 1-6), are all meditations on the Last Judgement and on the sickness and death which preceded that Judgement. Now as I said, you can read a very simple treatment of this in Helen Gardner's edition in part I of her introduction, where you will find a full explanation of the meditation as a religious exercise. As I said further, the form used by Donne was given wide circulation by St. Ignatius Loyola in the 1540's in his book of Spiritual Exercises. The idea is to use all the powers of the soul, not just the highest power, in an act, first of all, of concentration on a particular scene, which is called composition of place. And then you found on that a petition which is related to the subject matter, and then a prayer. The idea is to use the memory as a storehouse of images, the imagination as a source of terror in the face of reality, and so on. Anyway, you can read the account given by Helen Gardner in her introduction.

You can see that the sonnet is not wholly suitable for use as a composite exercise in meditation, but it has one great virtue, as Donne practises it anyway in this set; that is, it has a very strong break between the octave and the sestet — the break that is called the "volta," or turn. Donne uses that sharp break very often between the two sections. He uses the first eight lines, or the octave, as the composition of place, as an imaginative reconstruction, of his own death bed, for example, or the End of the World, the Day of Judgement; and then he changes the tone completely in the sestet and founds a prayer on it. So on the whole the octaves tend to be rather quieter, more contemplative. Look at No. 4 (Grierson's No. 7), which is a very famous one:

At the round earth's imagin'd corners, blow
Your trumpets, Angells, and arise, arise
From death, you numberlesse infinities
Of soules, and to your scattered bodies goe,

All whom the flood did, and the fire shall o'erthrow,
All whom warre, dearth, age, agues, tyrannies,
Despaire, law, chance, hath slaine, and you whose eyes
Shall behold God, and never tast deaths a woe.
But let them sleepe, Lord, and mee mourne a space,
For, if above all these, my sinnes abound,
'Tis late to aske abundance of thy grace,
When wee are there; here on this lowly ground,
Teach mee how to repent; for that's as good
As if thou'hadst seal'd my pardon, with thy blood.

Now that's a picture of the end of everything and you can see Donne, characteristically, wants to get everybody in. All these souls have been lying around and waiting for the day of Resurrection to be rejoined with their bodies. All have been separated from their bodies and there is a list of things that do tend to separate souls from bodies: flood, war, fire, famine, old age, fevers, tyrannies, so-called justice considered as an agent of death, despair, suicides, law (again the law), chance (accidents). That pretty well covers everything, but there is another class of people who are not covered by all that and that is the one group who do not taste death's woe, the people who are alive at the time of the Second Coming (Donne was very interested in this group and often mentions them in his sermons); so that everybody who has ever died and everybody who has ever lived who has not died — in other words, everybody — that is what the octave is really saying there. It's not a very clearly visualized picture of the Last Day. Even the opening lines are characteristic of Donne. He wants an heraldic picture of angels blowing trumpets in the corners of an apocalyptic scene; but he remembers that the world is round so he gets it all in in four words, the "round earths imagin'd corners." There is that play, still, of wit.

Then in the second part the tone is deliberately lowered. It simply says, don't let me get to that point or I shall be in dreadful trouble, because — and he refers to the bit in St. Paul about "grace abounding," that sin should not flourish that grace may abound — my own sins are greater than all these other people I've mentioned and therefore I need "grace abounding" before the Last Day; in other words, now. Before I can have it, of course, I must be taught repentance; I must repent before I can have forgiveness, and this is the old theological line: you can't get grace by repenting until you've had grace to repent, so what he's really asking for is what is called technically "prevenient grace" — the grace that softens the heart and enables repentance and therefore gives access to grace; the grace that Adam receives at the beginning of Book XI of *Paradise Lost*. Anyway, that's a very characteristic poem of Donne's at this period and it's clear that people tend to remember the octave more than the sestet.

The second sequence of six is a bit different and it is rather harder to describe that sequence as one of meditations. However, they do speak of atonement, and of the love which a man owes both to God and to his neighbour, and they plead for the intervention of God in the life of the subject. The most famous of these, I suppose, is "Batter my heart, three person'd God;" No. 10 (Grierson's No. 14). This is worth a word. He is asking God to take him by storm, treating himself as a town that is besieged by a liberator —

I, like a usurpt towne, to'another due,
Labour to'admit you, but Oh, to no end.

That's because the captain who should be in charge of the garrison, namely reason, has been captured and the Devil is running it. Then the military figure ends at line 8, that is to say at the end of the octave, and passes to a very different one, which is a marital figure — from martial to marital, if you like:

Yet dearely I love you, and would be loved faine,
But am betroth'd unto your enemie:
Divorce mee, 'untie, or breake that knot againe,
Take mee to you, imprison mee, for I
Except you'enthrall mee, never shall be free,
Nor ever chast, except you ravish mee.

The "enemie" (line 7) is, of course, the Devil. You see it becomes openly sexual at the end, as it often does in Donne's religious poetry. There's a very curious figure — Christ as a sort of complacent husband, opening the Church to all men, the Church being his wife. Here again you have got this break. The forced, meditative excitement of the first eight lines, "Batter my heart, three person'd God" — one imagines the Trinity actually battering on the door; and then he switches to the second part of the poem with this humble plea again.

I won't say anything on the other *Holy Sonnets*. The Sonnet on the death of his wife, in the Westmoreland Manuscript it is No. 1 (Grierson's No. 17), is rather famous, but not, I think, a very good poem. In fact it's extremely flat and laboriously worked out.

There are other poems which I won't speak of. *The Litanie,* which is the longest of the Divine Poems, I suppose, is not very notable. *The Crosse* you ought to look at; it's an anti-puritanical poem, in a way, but it's more interesting because of the way it shows you again the meditative aspect of Donne — the concentration on a particular figure which is worked out to the farthest possible extent. He finds crosses everywhere:

Who can deny mee power, and liberty
To stretch mine armes, and mine owne Crosse to be?

Swimme, and at every stroake, thou art thy Crosse;
The Mast and yard make one, where seas do tosse. . .

And then he finds that birds represent crosses; the meridians and parallels on a map represent crosses and so on. There's this same kind of imaginative concentration on an emblem or figure, getting all you can out of it. Here it is concentrated on one object, while in *The Calme* or *The Storme* it is very much more diffuse.

I've spoken before of the interest people felt at this time in what we should dismiss as simple coincidences; for example, the ubiquity of crosses in one form or another. One of Donne's poems is founded on what we should dismiss as a calendrical coincidence; *Upon the Annuntiation and Passion Falling upon one Day. 1608.* That occasionally happens. Lady Day, which is the day of the Annunciation, is the 25th of March, and it's not altogether surprising that Good Friday should occasionally fall on that date too. But for Donne the coincidence of these two falling on the same date is the occasion for another meditation on these significant overlaps, these analogies — the world is really made that way — as we see all through his poetry.

The best of these occasional poems is genuinely an occasional one. It's the one called *Good Friday, 1613. Riding Westward,* which does appear to have been written, as we gather from manuscript titles, when he was on the way to see Edward Herbert in Wales. It's a sort of horse-back poem. It's again a typical meditation and, again, on one of those paradoxes; Good Friday's the day when everyone is meant to be facing Eastward, so to speak, but he is riding westward and has his back to the East. It's all founded on that, but it starts off with an elaborate astronomical figure which goes on for ten lines of the poem and then becomes much simpler:

Yet dare I'almost be glad, I do not see
That spectacle of too much weight for mee.
Who sees Gods face, that is selfe life, must dye;
What a death were it then to see God dye?

A very strange double rhyme there, called a "rime riche" in French, but not often used in English — it is very strong, I think, at that point. And then the meditation continues, working out the idea that his back is turned to the East so that people will see correction. Corrections will

Burne off my rusts, and my deformity,

and it will "Restore thine Image." When that's been done, when his deformities are removed, then he will turn to the East. Again, by modern standards, the occasion of that poem, the way it is worked out, might strike one as trivial, but in fact it's very much a theme of its time.

The *Lamentations of Jeremy* are not very interesting. A word about the three *Hymnes*, the *Hymne to Christ at the Authors Last Going into Germany* and the *Hymne to God my God, in my Sicknesse*, and *A Hymne to God the Father*. The first presumably belongs to 1619. The other two were probably both written in 1623 during his illness. The *Hymne to God the Father* is really rather simple. It is a hymn — Donne wrote it to be set to music, which it was — and according to Walton he often had it played in St. Paul's.

The *Hymne to God, my God, in my Sicknesse* is a much more complicated poem and presumably the last of Donne's important, witty poems. It starts off with the figure of himself preparing to join the heavenly "quire" by tuning his instrument before the door, preparing for death. And then that musical figure changes abruptly, as often in the secular poems, to a figure from geography.

Whilst my Physitians by their love are growne
   Cosmographers, and I their Mapp, who lie
Flat on this bed, that by them may be showne
   That this is my South-West discoverie
Per fretum febris, by these streights to die,
   I joy, that in these streights I see my West;

You see what's going on. The doctors pore over him, as geographers pore over a map. They're looking not for a North-West passage, but for a South-West passage. West was the orientation of decline and South was that of heat; he was dying of a fever. Through the straits of fever, from which he will pass out of this life, he sees his West. Then he says it's just as well to go West as East, because East and West come together on the map; and so death and resurrection come together. Then he meditates where "home," namely Paradise, is; is it in any of these places?

All streights, and none but streights, are wayes to them,
   Whether where *Japhet* dwelt, or *Cham,* or *Sem*. . .

These sons of Noah were said to have founded the three main divisions of the human race; Cham, for instance, was the father of the Negroes. Then there is another switch from the Biblical figure to the myth that Calvary was on the same location as Paradise; and to the familiar figure of the first and the second Adam.

Well, it's a difficult poem, but again I think we can see certain continuities with the younger Donne. Continuities exist, but differences exist too. On the whole there is less variety, less matter for thought, probably, than in the greatest of the *Songs and Sonnets,* but that of course is something that concerns only us. It wasn't of very much concern to his contemporaries.

VIII

MILTON: *PARADISE LOST I*

KENNETH PALMER

I want to speak about *Paradise Lost,* but I must also touch on one or two points about Milton himself, which help show what kind of poet he was. He was a learned and dedicated poet; he was an humanist; a Christian — a puritan Christian; and he was a Platonist and an idealist. This is quite apart, of course, from those things which took up his time as Latin Secretary during the Commonwealth. I want to explain what these terms mean.

He was an humanist in the strict sense; he was passionately devoted, that is to say, to Greek and Latin literature and to the ideas they embodied, the political as well as the literary ones. That implies an admiration for Republican ideals which goes along with commitment to liberty of conscience. You might expect to find this in a poet who lived after the Reformation, and it helps to explain why Milton showed a strong desire for reform in both Church and State. Milton was also temperamentally an optimist and an idealist, and he believed in the gradual improvement of man and his lot on Earth, which is why he thought it was worth pursuing reform in Church and State. It means that he would have sided with people like Bacon, for example, rather than with people like Donne. (He wrote early a Latin poem, *Naturam non pati senium,* on the theme that nature does not suffer from old age and decay.)

He was an humanist also in respect of what that implies in people like Roger Ascham. It meant that you imitated the best models in classical literature for your own purposes. You imitated because you knew that you were working within a tradition, and you wished that to be known because it allowed you and your reader much more richness and flexibility in your effects. If the reader knew generally the terms in which you were working, then a variation from what he expected had a much more potent effect on him.

To be an humanist and a Protestant tended to make you a man of serious moral conviction and, as a writer, to evince a strong religious strain — as, of course, you find is the case with Spenser. That is something which can also be connected with Plato and Platonism. Plato himself was a kind of puritan in both moral and literary matters, as you can see from his discussion of poetry in *The Republic*. He was a favourite philosopher with Puritans (Peter Sterry, who was Cromwell's chaplain, was a noted Platonic scholar). Aristotle was thought of as being old-fashioned and medieval, because he had strongly influenced the Schoolmen and thus the whole structure of Catholic theology. But he represented, also, simply the old-fashioned education. Milton, when at Cambridge, was very sarcastic about the syllabus.

Milton's learning was, of course, considerable. He was scholarly from his early teens: we know that he sat up until midnight or after, (with a maid to ensure he didn't stay too long). He was a noted scholar at the University and a good linguist and poet as a young man. His travels in Italy encouraged him to produce poems in Italian as well as in Latin. And, of course, there was that prolonged and highly disciplined period of reading at Horton, which he undertook to make himself a professional poet.

He could, in fact, have been a professional scholar, even by the standards of our own century, but of course he became Latin Secretary, and a controversialist too. He was conscious of the need for learning, first to raise the status of poetry in an age which had grown more learned and self-aware in Europe, and secondly to prepare for his major work, especially the epic, which was thought of as the greatest production of the human mind and which required a command of all human erudition: a notion which persisted in English literature as late as the time of Coleridge.

He found it necessary to defend himself against his father. He hadn't produced anything to justify a large investment of time and money, and his father was, not unnaturally, feeling a bit anxious. But Milton wanted no other profession: poetry was the only goal he had. (That explains the sonnet:

How soon hath Time, the subtle thief of youth,

Stol'n on his wing my three and twentieth year!

and, also, next year, the Latin poem, *Ad Patrem,* in which he justifies himself for waiting). It's of course difficult to explain your dedication to an art when you haven't anything at all to show for it, in comparison with those "timely happy spirits," as Milton called them, who had produced something earlier. (He may have had in mind somebody like Thomas Randolph, or more likely Abraham Cowley, who published work apparently written at the age of thirteen).

Learning, and imitation, and serious regard for the art of poetry, are interlinked. In one way the poet was joined with all his predecessors and learned from them and used them, so that he was rather like a man who accepted a traditional church and traditional doctrine and authority.

If you wrote in English, however, you felt (even after the achievement of Shakespeare) apprehensive about writing in the vernacular. The vernacular still needed, that is, an authority of its own; it hadn't yet finally established itself. And you still had to apply to English what you knew to be right from your studies in Latin and Greek. So you had two tasks: first, to translate the lessons of classical literature into the vernacular mode and, secondly, to use in its turn the literature of England for imitation – just as one would have used the classics themselves; so that Milton uses Shakespeare and Spenser as well as many minor poets of his own era. To perform these tasks rightly you needed not only learning but a sense of authority. You were the final judge and keeper of your own poetic conscience.

Now if that should be your view of poetry, it's a very much of a piece with being a Puritan – not with being a kill-joy, that is, but with being an independent, somebody who felt strongly anti-prelatic. You are yourself your own final court of appeal. You have no one to help you with your poetry any more than you have to help you with your devotions. There's no priest standing between you and the object of your worship. That is probably why the young Milton, in his *Vacation Exercise,* excuses English by comparison with Latin, but justifies it, nevertheless, as being fit for the naked thoughts he has which need to be both brought forth and clothed. It also explains why, even so early, Milton thought it proper to assume so assured and lofty a tone.

From the first he chose to be elevated. T.S. Eliot said, not very kindly, that Milton had elected a perch from which he cannot afford to fall and from which he's in danger of slipping. It might be fairer to say that Milton isn't perched at all, but that he's making English try something new. He's using in English the long-breathed and musical patterns of syntax that he associated with the Italian poets, while still keeping firmly to the native English qualities of sound and sense. His power lies, as he put it, in trying to "build the lofty rhyme" while still exploiting all the possibilities of English rhythm, and syntax, and of course, vocabulary.

His assurance comes partly from his own nature, partly from his learning and his conscious dedication to his art, and partly from his optimistic view of history. It would, of course, make him slightly vulnerable to anybody who chose to take the other view. Donne, for example, who believed that the world was decaying, was, like Chaucer, convinced that man was a mixture of good and evil, and that no Utopian scheme would ever work. Milton, at least while he was young, and certainly for some time during the Commonwealth, supposed that man might be improved. This view was perhaps inevitable for a Neo-Platonist, who has always argued the way of ascent and perfection, so that, although properly a Christian, Milton might be tempted to speak as if no Fall of Man had ever occurred. One can see here a form of the millenial hope of the Puritans. As they perceived it, the Renaissance had restored the purity of Latin style, as against the ignorance of the Middle Ages, and the Reformation had purified the corruption of doctrine and practice, so that it only needed to depose the bishops, and probably kings, to usher in the rule of the saints and the Kingdom of Christ on Earth.

Some critics say, when Milton refers to the "late fantastics," that they know which poets it is he's objecting to, but they have never satisfactorily been identified: "trimming slight" doesn't really sound like Donne and, of course, it may have been some minor Cambridge group. Perhaps the question doesn't seem very important, but fundamentally it is, because Milton was defending *his* method, which implies that he had a choice open to him, and one is forced to ask what choice there was. It's usually assumed that he reacted against people like Donne, or perhaps Jonson, and their followers, but of course most of those poets didn't publish until 1633 or after; their poems circulated in manuscript. The poets who were in print were followers of Spenser, and it's primarily Spenser whom Milton himself follows: sometimes by allusion or imitation, sometimes by his methods and his purpose, as we can see from the *Areopagitica*, where he refers to our "sage and serious poet Spenser, whom I dare be known to think a better teacher than Scotus or Aquinas", following that with an allusion to Guyon at the Cave of Mammon. Dryden said that Milton had acknowledged to him that Spenser was his original.

There's the further point that the poets following Donne and Jonson were largely amateurs, but Milton was always a poet and nothing else. He was like Jonson in his devotion to his art, although what supports him is not Horace, but Hebraism and Platonism.

It is true that the young Milton had attempted witty poetry, but a comparison with other writers of short witty poems will show you an important and rather paradoxical difference.

If you take Donne as your example, then you have a Christian who was a

IX

MILTON: *PARADISE LOST II*

KENNETH PALMER

We made the approach to Paradise, as everybody points out, by way of Satan. Necessarily, in this poem, all the blessedness, except that which belongs peculiarly to Heaven, has to be seen through fallen eyes. Paradise, the earthly garden of blessedness, is a type of types (and some of those types we have already had suggested on Satan's journey down from the outside of the Cosmos), but it also contains within it a number of psychological symbols. It is, amongst other things, the supreme form of sexual pleasure, as well as a kind of return to the womb. But all the delights that it represents and embodies are modified; they're all ordered, in due course, because although all the bodily pleasures are there in full, they are perfectly regulated, and they are subordinated, oddly enough, to the order of the mind, as we can see from the instructions that Raphael gives to Adam, after Adam has accounted for his creation and the delight that he takes in Eve.

In some ways Paradise is like other literary gardens. (There was, after all, one in Ariosto's *Orlando Furioso;* there was one in Dante's *Purgatorio*, which was far above the atmosphere, and therefore, being beyond the sphere of the moon, beyond change). But it's not just another *locus amoenus,* it is also (and the steep cliff and the high wall around it suggest this) an *hortus conclusus,* and that leads us to two different things. First and probably the more important is the *Canticles* (iv. 12), ("A garden enclosed is my sister, my spouse, a spring shut up, a fountain sealed.") and Milton draws on the *Canticles* elsewhere in this poem. (In Book V, Adam awakens Eve with echoes of the *Canticles,* and there are memories of its rich fruits and flowers and scents throughout the description of the Garden. There is also the allegorical relationship (and one mustn't forget it), implicit in the *Canticles*, of Christ to His Church). Secondly, the *hortus conclusus* was a symbol for the Virgin Mary, who was of course the second Eve, and this is explicit in the fifth Book:

> On whom the Angel "Hail"
> Bestowed, the holy salutation used
> Long after to blest Mary, second Eve.

v. 385-7

The lavishness of the garden and the natural bounty of Eve lead us to the celebration of fruitfulness. The garden is copious; it includes in itself all kinds; Adam and Eve see that it is beyond their capacity to control. But Eve herself is the "mother of all mankind", she is the woman whose

> fruitful womb
> Shall fill the world more numerous with thy sons
> Than with these various fruits the trees of God
> Have heaped this table.

v. 388-91

That not only ties up with the constant allusions to eating and fruit and feasts and banquets in the poem, but also with human and spiritual sexuality. The angels in some sense "know" each other — Raphael says so in Book V. Perhaps what is more important is that the Fallen Angels *can't* know each other; they are loveless and sterile. It is significant that although her intentions were good when she suggested it, it is fallen Eve who implies that willed sterility might avert the effects of original sin. Such an act has the same effect as want of love, and this, of course, is what Milton points out. After the Fall, love was lost, both of God and of each other.

The trees in the Garden are of all kinds, as *Genesis* explained, and it's just the same in Dante's garden. This is necessary because perfection consists in the completeness; (it *is* completeness). The catalogue of trees is commonplace in literature; it's present in three different books in Spenser, it's in Chaucer, and in the *Aeneid.* The fullness and scale of the Garden, its power to exceed whatever you can imagine, is apparent even as you approach it with Satan. You have first of all something like Pope's "Alps on Alps" formula; you look "up the verdurous wall" and it seems to stretch an enormous distance. Then, quite suddenly, your point of view is changed, and you look downwards, as if from Adam's position. It's a double over-going of expectation.

The trees above the wall excel by their quality and their luxuriance, but also by the fact that they bear both fruit and flower at the same time. It's rather like what the explorers of the New World were excited by in the orange — Herbert comments upon it and so does Marvell. They thought the New World was an unfallen world; it was our earthly paradise. This coincidence of seasons is commonplace in earthly paradises, but it's necessary here for simple astronomical and meteorological reasons.

The allusions and the comparisons that are used in this part of the poem work in a number of ways: some of them work primarily for Paradise, and some for Satan. Because we can, at the same time, apprehend Paradise and know something of the nature of the Fallen Angels, we see things in both ways, rather as, physically, Milton makes us look both up to Paradise and down again from the top. The scents of the Garden recall merchant ships and spices, the winds from *Arabia felix,* and we remember Satan, like "a fleet descried," in Book II, long before he even reached Hell's Gate. The "spicy drugs" (ii. 640) link up with the spicy scents and flavour of the fruit of the tree (iv. 156ff). Satan, of course, is filled not with anything good, but with "mischievous revenge". In the Garden he is entertained with these "odorous sweets" as well as with the intense purity of the air.

The goodness of the Garden does not prevent Satan from trying to destroy it; he soars over the wall, prowls like a wolf and perches like a cormorant. These similes compare him with the hirelings in the Church, picking up hints both from *Lycidas* and from Christ's parable. (It's natural for Milton to compare Satan both with the priesthood and the episcopacy; false reason destroys natural good, and that was how Milton saw Church government. It also leads to other allusions — there's a pun in Book X, referring to the tremendous bridge built by Sin and Death, joining Hell and Earth: it was done by "wondrous art *pontifical"*).

The fruitfulness and the fertility is further developed in the description of the rivers, which are also the Cardinal Virtues. The sapphire fount is the Wisdom which underlies all the virtues. You ought to notice here that the waters run "with mazy error" (iv. 239). If that's rather surprising, you should recall that this is before the Fall and that a word like "error" means what it originally meant, i.e., wandering. Words appear purged in the Garden; they are *potentially* fallen, just as Adam and Eve may be, and once or twice they seem dangerously poised, but they haven't yet toppled over.

A fortiori, the Garden makes the fiend "stupidly good" — even he can recall half his unfallen nature — and the notion of fallen nature brings us back to the old argument of the pastoral. This Garden is related to all sorts of images of the unfallen and perfect state, and, as in other pastorals, nature has to precede art because art is only needed to make good what is wanting in fallen nature. Nature here appears to be overcoming art on art's own terms. It's rather like the language poets used to describe a perfect, unfallen, natural world, using the terms of art to do it. Marvell in *Bermudas* refers to the Spring which "enamells" everything. But, of course, for fallen man, art has to be the medium by which he embodies that perfect nature. Milton hints at what art could do if there were any necessity for it — "to tell how, if Art could tell" (iv. 236) or flowers "which not nice Art ... but Nature boon/Poured forth profuse." (iv. 241-3). This is a technique similar to that which Milton uses when he's employing myth or mythical comparisons. Referring to the golden apples he talks about "Hesperian fables true,/If true, here only." (iv. 250-1); just as, contrariwise, he refers to the legend of Mulciber in Book I, who according to classical myth was "thrown ... o'er the crystal battlements," and then adds "Thus they relate,/Erring" because, of course, Milton knows he "fell" much earlier.

Because nature is dominant, because there's no need for art, it is possible constantly to allude to art. You don't get flower beds and "curious knots" in this Garden, but at the same time, because Paradise represents what art later tried to recreate, Milton can safely refer to the landscape-making of the seventeenth century, which started with the painters and became the peculiarly English complement to the Palladian country house. Adam's abode is the apotheosis of the "happy rural seat" of various country squires.

Nature and art can, of course, be quite subtly combined, as they are in the complicated pun on "vernal airs" (iv. 264ff), (which is discussed at some length by Ricks in *Milton's Grand Style*). Nature, however, because it's utterly unfallen, is better than art; it can improve on what art later knows. Milton is able to allude to the rose which is without thorns (although, of course, he didn't know about Chinese roses, which are so). What matters to him is the symbolic quality, the state of grace it represents. For the Middle Ages, the rose had its own peculiar symbolism: the *rosa sine spina* was the Blessed Virgin.

When Adam and Eve appear, and Satan sees them, and we see them through Satan, Milton makes three points about them: they are godlike, they are majestic, and they are naked. They're god-like because they are the epitome of various attempts to depict the Greek gods, both in language and in the plastic arts. They embody, however, details from other sources. The length of the hair, for example, comes largely from Biblical texts. (There's some indication that Adam is like the sun-god, Apollo: his lack of beard perhaps would suggest this, although Adam wasn't always clean-shaven in paintings). They're majestic, not only because they epitomize all regal qualities, but also because they are potentially King and Queen of the whole human race. It's a paradox to say so because we can't help thinking of them as being primitive, although the rest of the poem makes it quite clear that they are very sophisticated. That paradox is present, too, in the notion of their nakedness. They are naked, but they're clad in native honour. In seventeenth-century poetic Gardens "honour" had no place: it was a monster that was a deterrent to fruition. But this Garden is quite the contrary. It may be representative of all such Gardens, but it contains true honour. We know from the VIIIth Book, when Adam described his first meeting with Eve, "she what was honour knew,/And with obsequious majesty approved/ My pleaded reason." (508-10).

I want to touch briefly on one or two other topics, and first, on the notion of order and the patterns of symmetry that appear throughout the poem and are part of what the poem is celebrating. If we look at Adam's account of his own creation in Book VIII, for example, we get a strong sense that he's improvising a conversation, trying to keep Raphael. This is, of course, important for Milton's purposes because it leads on to a crucial discussion about right rule and hierarchy, and the risk of submission through the power of the senses to Eve who is his inferior; but the improvisation also relates back to what God himself seems to do. He knows that He's going to create Eve, but He plays a game with Adam and lets Adam persuade Him to it. That is how Adam must see God's foreknowledge, even though he may be face to face with God.

When Adam makes his plea for Eve, he bases it on notions of order and decorum, saying that there can be no real society amongst unequals, that love should be morally restrained and balanced. The unfallen Adam is all temperance, just as the world that he lives in is itself in perfect "temper" — a musical as well as a medical term. For this reason, says Adam, he can have no company with the brutes. He argues, quite naturally, from music; he refers to harmony or "true delight mutual, in proportion due,/Given and received." (viii. 385-6). The proportion that has to be kept reminds us of Richard II's meditation in prison, when he reflects on his own failure to keep any kind of hierarchy or balance. Adam wants "all rational delight" — *rational* is the key word — and therefore he says animals can't be "consort" (and "consort" is itself another musical term). Adam makes the right plea and he gets his way, or so it seems to him.

This argues a kind of mathematical and musical order in the Creation; it's Pythagorean or Platonic, and it's not surprising to find that in the first edition of the poem, Adam's story is itself part of a numerical symmetry. (That edition of the poem had ten Books and therefore Adam's account was in Book VII, three Books from the end. Eve's account of her creation was in Book IV, three Books from the beginning. She too uses the same ambiguous term, "consort").

All things in the Garden appear in a number of ways: what they are and have been, and what they might be, fallen; and this applies most of all to the idea of knowledge. Adam, in Books V-VIII, can have knowledge of almost everything he asks for, including knowledge of various kinds of fall, of the genesis and forms of evil, and even a prophetic allusion to the destructive tendency in fallen creatures – he knows, by Raphael's narration, of the invention of artillery in Heaven, which, of course, looks forward to what man himself will do. But from Book IX onwards, his knowledge is of what ultimately will be, and of change in himself and Eve. He learns what death will mean and, even more poignantly, of what might have come to pass had he not fallen. He had been given hints of what might yet be, but he was warned to remain content with what was. When he is fallen, he finds out that Paradise might have been his capital seat but that now it will certainly be destroyed. It will become an island "salt and bare, The haunt of seals and orcs, and sea-mews' clang." (xi. 834-5), an epitome of complete desolation and loss. Everything that Adam had hitherto taken as naturally good now turns wrong and sour. The weather and the seasons change because the fallen world changes its astronomy and therefore its meteorology; the weather turns thundery at the completion of the "mortal sin original." Proper relationship with the brute creation also goes. It's interesting that Satan anticipates all this when he's orbiting the Earth in darkness; he takes a course which is technically possible only in a fallen universe. When, too, he wants to spy on Adam and Eve, and wishes to disguise himself as predatory beasts, he makes each beast suspicious and angry and dangerous – in fact, fallen.

Adam learns after the Fall that his act of eating the apple has destroyed every proportion, every harmony, every aspect of order in his world, from his own marriage in the centre right out to the edge of the Cosmos. He knows that the possibility of growing up to spirit, which was what Raphael hinted to him in Book V, has now been reversed. The original growth was bound to be stopped if any creature were to try either for knowledge which wasn't proper to it, which might lead to contradiction or nonsense – as indeed it does in the arguments between Satan and Eve when she falls – or for a position which wasn't natural to it.

Satan, and Eve, in rejecting hierarchy, move both into psychological and theological disorder, and into contradiction: they deny their origin. Consequently, they upset all the other relationships that they know. Eve, who would not accept a proper relationship with Adam, finishes by bowing to a mere tree. We should remember, too, that the Serpent says that, having tasted the tree, he proceeded to "speculation high" – precisely the sort of thing that Raphael warned Adam to leave alone. The more intellectual of the fallen angels in Hell occupy their time in just the same way, with questions of freewill, foreknowledge, and astronomy. It's no accident that all the things that we know as being natural to us must, in the poem, be very largely acted out for us by the devils. It's they who inaugurate formal debates, invent the process of scientific inquiry, produce elaborate architecture, recognise the need for theatrical self-projection in asserting oneself, and know the sweetness of attempting revenge.

The dangerous inversion of hierarchy, both moral and psychological, was hinted at in Book VIII with the account by Adam just before the Fall. Adam tells Raphael that he was delighted by the pleasures of the Garden, but not altered by them; his senses didn't overpower him. When he met Eve, however, all his senses were upset, including the sense of touch; he says he was transported: "here passion first I felt." For this he is promptly rebuked by Raphael. Adam makes it clear that reason falls before the presence of Eve; wisdom, he says, "like folly shows." This is exactly the argument of Berowne to Rosaline in *Love's Labour's Lost*. It is, of course, what happens at the Fall, in Book IX.

Adam has no one to envy within the human universe, and therefore what happens to him is an inversion of his normal state; his affections lead him to do something that he ought not to do. What happens to Eve, who *can* envy, is an assertion of her ambition. At her fall she adopts the language of a person whom, in his own age, Milton must have found peculiarly intolerable — the petulant, fashionable fine lady, whom we know from Restoration comedy. Unfortunately Adam too takes up a similar pose when he has eaten the fruit, and he congratulates Eve on her nice judgement — "Eve, now I see thou art exact of taste,/ And elegant, of sapience no small part." (ix. 1017-8). They move all the way from the first week of the Creation down to the end of the seventeenth century in a few seconds.

X

MILTON: *PARADISE LOST III*

KENNETH PALMER

Paradise Lost, even as a title, implies not merely narrative, but structural, charcteristics of the poem: not only the loss, the woe, the state of man's fall, but also Paradise itself, the state of being unfallen — the condition as well as the place. This is partly presented by direct means, and partly available to us, fallen men, by negation and contrast. In some sense, the formula Paradise Lost is the most succesful way available to us for talking about Paradise. *Paradise Lost* is at least as much about perfection and joy as it is about sin and death and "all our woe."

Milton uses Biblical story (which for him was essentially the literal truth); but because of the nature of the story, and the nature of poetry, it is convenient for us to talk, as critics do, about Milton's myth. Now this is not an evasion. It brings us back to earlier critical discussions of the divided sensibility of the later seventeenth century. Milton is trying to present in this poem something which only myth can adequately attempt: something for which logical analysis or the exercise of discursive reason — everything you can think of as appropriate to the reason since the seventeenth century — is not really adequate. His myth does, by its nature, what, in shorter poems, is done by metaphor. And that is the reason, I suppose, why Milton's language is less metaphoric than, say, Shakespeare's and why he uses very little allegory.

If you read Isabel MacCaffrey's excellent book you'll find that she argues that the images of the myth are the reality. Myth, which is a way of dealing with complexity, may be primitive, in the sense that it deals with something quite fundamental in our natures, and may appear to be primitive in the way in which we think of art itself as a primitive form, but it is not therefore, in its effect, unsophisticated. Meaning in myth is summed up or embodied in great "simple" figures or actions. (That is why Rosemond Tuve, in *Images and Themes in Five Poems by Milton,* made so much of the basic images in the early poems: Milton is consistent in his aesthetic). Analysis is a method later than myth, and one which destroys the effect peculiar to myth — which is not to say that one cannot talk about poems which use myth. Owen Barfield once proposed a view of poetic language which made it analogous to myth. According to him, words in primitive language may present merely (as later people say) names of things; but if you say that, then you must also say that the things themselves were more than merely the material objects. (This is the kind of argument that Ruskin used about Greek mythology in respect of woods and rivers and so forth; the Greeks could hardly think of trees without thinking of Dryads as well — Tree-plus-Dryad-inhabiting-it). In later language the meanings split up into abstract and concrete, subjective and objective, particular and general.

When Milton says, as he does in the treatise *On Education,* that by comparison with logical discourse, poetry is "more simple, sensuous, and passionate," he means, first, that poetry operates not only by mere reason, but through the feelings and senses — which is effectually what Barfield said — and, secondly, that the images of poetry are simple rather in the sense that God is simple (in scholastic terminology): that is to say, they are not divisible but fully integrated; like God, they are beings without parts, whole and entire.

Milton's whole effort in *Paradise Lost* is to use the means available to fallen man (his fragmented universe, his analytic mind and language, his logical methods) to create an image of unfallen man in his Paradise. He attempts to take up all the images, the likenesses, and, if necessary, the unlikenesses, which will allow themselves to be subsumed into the single wholeness of whatever form of perfection he is trying to mediate. The similes, the types, the parallels, the "sub-plot" of Satan, what Johnson called "retrospection and anticipation" — all these serve this end.

Now *Paradise Lost* has a structure in time, though with an action which is not confined by time; but space is also important, and morally significant, within it. The narrative doubles back on itself. It looks forward and backwards and alludes to other times and places. Only part of it deals with Paradise, and that part looks all ways at once. (Unexpectedly the place of the enclosed bower and the unfallen pair is the place of the telling of the most violent parts of the poem).

Milton has some of the advantages of drama. There is a three level "stage", such as he had for the masque at Ludlow; there is action, choral commentary where necessary, and omniscient spectators in heaven. Some of the characteristics belong to more stylized forms of drama — the "moral levels" of the *Comus* situation, — and some to anachronistic modes, as you have in medieval cycles, where past and future are implicit in the present moment. But Milton also gives himself full freedom of narrative as well. That is to say, he enjoyed what the late A. J. A. Waldock denied him: the novelist's privilege of using dramatic incident within a more flexible but less "immediate" medium.

God alone, in this poem, knows exactly what is happening, since to Him, in Eliot's phrase, "all time is eternally present." (I can only try to explain his paradox about Time by another concerning Space. If you think of Mercator's projection of the globe, you see a point (that is, the North Pole) represented as a line, parallel to and as long as the Equator. Anyone, at any point on the Equator, looks due North to the Pole, which is really a point, but on this map is a line — a point infinitely extended. In respect of Time, this is God's position with reference to finite creatures.) But when God is directly present in the poem, we also, as far as language will allow it, — and the language does its best — are able to see with His "eyes." We can move freely, (and the syntax tries to encourage us to do it), into past and future, free of prejudice. In the rest of the poem it is quite frequently through Satan's eyes that we look, at least until after the Fall; from that point on, we can see through the eyes of Adam and Eve. It's over Satan's shoulder, if you like, that we see "undelighted, all delight." (iv. 286). We can follow arguments, and associate ourselves with positions of which we needn't approve rationally, and with which we can sympathise in our own persons — the resentment, the envy, the desire for revenge, as motives. We, (and not merely Satan) bring evil with us to contaminate something which, intellectually, we acknowledge as a good. As we go further, we become gradually involved with our own kind, though we begin, in the poem, by seeing them as other than ourselves. Recognition comes later. It's quite a shock to find that the two "of far nobler shape" are human. We see very much as Satan sees: to him the first love-making in Paradise is a matter of envy; and envy is precisely what brought about his own fall, and will later bring down Eve.

Time in the poem is, despite the Divine freedom, precisely defined, although Milton's manipulation of it destroys the reader's sense of linear continuity. Even in those Books where the action passes on Earth, the Time of the unfallen world is felt as something both regular and circular. (Heaven also, as Gabriel says, knows analogies to Earth's day and night, for "vicissitude"). Earth has all seasons in one; fruit and flower come together; perpetual equinox gives perpetual spring.

The movement of the action, in effect, is from Hell by way of Paradise, up to Heaven and the War of the Angels; then by way of the Creation down to the Fall and so to our present level. All acts within the poem are seen spatially, and space has moral implications. (We are sometimes forced to use such spatial terms, saying that God is outside time; and Milton uses them of Satan —

> From what highth fall'n

or

> In the lowest deep a lower deep
> Still threatening to devour me opens wide.)

This is something which corresponds to our normal use of the language, but it's something which is quite fundamental to Milton's method).

Further, the "double" narrative — the fact that great events are usually seen in more than one way, or are described on more than one occasion, as in an epistolary novel — gives what are quite literally different points of view. This is a matter of spatial shift, not merely from one person's psychological and moral peculiarities to another's but from one part of the universe to another, with all that that implies about the point of origin of the person who sees. The rebel angels and the faithful angels look from different places, which are themselves different moral and psychological positions. Consequently, the main action of the poem creates, or defines, its whole universe, both physically and spiritually. What God sees when He's looking at Satan in orbit round the Cosmos, and foresees, (and narrates), is really an episode (seeing Satan and his actions from a fresh point of view); but His first speech is also a sketch (an attempt to put theological first things first) of what the poem sets out at large. Adam's visions in Books XI and XII are analogues to what God sees always — minor "enactments" played out on a vast stage before him, but without any *temporal* implications. There's no process that he himself lives through. There are, of course, certain spatial correspondences throughout the poem. Satan goes up to Paradise; Sin and Death make their bridge from Hell up to Earth, in fact they go higher than Earth — they go up in a great arc and come down to the globe. The Son moves down to create the Cosmos, and then moves back again up to Heaven to rejoice in it and contemplate it. Satan, himself, in the whole action of the poem, follows a great arc but ends where he began.

Correspondences may go further. Opening the infernal debate, Satan argues:

> From this descent

Celestial Virtues rising will appear

More glorious and more dread than from no fall

ii. 14-16.

And that of course, is essentially the argument over the forbidden Tree and its fruit; but it's also a parody of the theological argument about the Fall and Redemption, the "felix culpa", the "necessarium peccatum Adae," the Fall of man which brings about a greater blessedness. (Significantly, the Redemption, unlike Satan's "celestial virtues," works by Grace, and not by diabolic self-help). Similarly, although Milton doesn't make full use in the poem of the concept of the Trinity, he does offer the diabolic parody of it. In Heaven, there is the Father, who begets the Son, and from both proceeds the Holy Ghost —

In Hell, one has instead —

As Mammon says on another occasion, Hell produces excellent imitations (And what can Heav'n show more? (ii. 273)). It can originate nothing of itself, except destruction.

XI

A FEW GENERAL NOTES
ON THE HEROIC POEM

KENNETH PALMER

Writing an heroic poem in the seventeenth century became difficult with the advent of a sceptical and scientific temper of mind. Poetry even began to be thought of as an inferior form, and traditional kinds of knowledge became suspect, particularly mythology. The disruption is quite clear as early as Bacon: there is a growing and rigorous control of what language can do, and a sceptical treatment of myth and fable, and a desire to use empirical methods of inquiry — although not all scientists in the seventeenth century were as empirical as all that.

Poetry was still admitted to contain, or embody, ancient wisdom, but there was no desire amongst the majority that poetry should continue to do this. Poets had always been skilful in hiding their secrets from the uninitiated, and poetry had always been something that needed a measure of translation if the vulgar were to understand it. The century believed it had better means of dealing with the sort of truths poetry was meant to convey. The Royal Society was quite clear that truth was accessible to its methods of inquiry; it wanted language to be of a mathematical plainness, it wanted "positive expressions" and clear senses. The problems examined were to be solved by the reduction or removal of most of what constitutes language. (The *reductio ad absurdum* of the whole thing to be found in Book III of *Gulliver's Travels,* where the learned men of Laputa carry around, or have carried around for them, bags of *things* with which they conduct their purely mimetic conversations).

You get a similar view of the relationship of poetry to the world of phenomena in seventeenth-century ideas of the role of rhetoric. The common-place notion of style as a garment is likely to be found when style is thought of as something purely detachable, where language is basically the medium plus the decoration. Hence the language of poets was allowed to deal with what is not; it dealt largely in similitudes which were not exact, because they primarily emphasized likeness. This aspect of poetry was labelled "fancy". But the mind has also to deal in unlikenesses, and that, of course, is the faculty of judgement. Judgement was always thought of as superior to fancy — you can see it discussed in the critical essays of Dryden — and the two together produced wit. That theory, which is found in Dryden, is based largely on Hobbes, especially his *Answer* to Davenant. (Surprisingly, it persists as late as Johnson — you may remember Johnson's remark about the "dangerous prevalence of the imagination").

In spite of this, the heroic poem still retained its reputation for supremacy among intellectual achievements and it continued to hold this poition, although nobody produced heroic poems in order to prove the theory. The idea is clearly expressed in Dryden's dedication of the *Aeneis* (1697), where he says it is the "greatest work that the soul of man is capable to perform." His reason is that although it is a fiction, its purpose is to instruct; its purpose is to "form the mind to heroic virtue by example." That, of course, is very close to Spenser's thesis for his own *Faerie Queene.*

Usually, and especially for the Renaissance poet, a work of this kind would be based on some event of national history. This was partly due to the influence of Homer and Virgil, and partly to the strongly nationalistic temper of Renaissance civilization. (It is very difficult to say how coherent medieval Christendom had been: Renaissance Christendom certainly wasn't). The notion of national history as a topic enabled the poet to begin, as he knew he ought, *in medias res:* that is, it enabled him to move both ways, forwards and backwards in time. It enabled him especially to move forwards, whether in dream or prophecy, so as to reflect glory on his own age. You could look forward to the age of the reigning sovereign and say how magnificent everything would be.

The heroic poem, therefore, was a kind of assertion of national maturity. It meant that everybody recognised that the nation had a history of some substance and worth, and that by this stage it had a language rich and copious enough to produce heroic poetry, poetry no longer barbarous, medieval and limited. In Italy you had Dante, Ariosto and Tasso; in France you had the attempts — rather than the achieved successes — of Ronsard; and in England you had the imperfect success of Spenser.

Milton's purpose was even loftier than that of Renaissance poets elsewhere. He put stronger emphasis than they did on the moral function of heroic poems. He speaks, in the *Reason of Church Government,* about virtue and public civility, and elsewhere about sanctity and virtue, with a corresponding stress on the inspiration of the Holy Spirit rather than the Muse or memory. That aligns the poet with the Apostles or the Hebrew prophets, and reminds us of the expectation that Christ's Second coming upon Earth was indeed imminent. But we have to remember that Milton is the last real writer of heroic poetry in English (for we can comfortably exclude people like Blackmore). The impulse to produce such poetry was transmuted after this, and the major poets produced either translations — Dryden of the *Aeneid,* and Pope of the *Iliad* — or else the mock heroic, a parodic development of the heroic poem.

The natural subject for an English heroic poet was the story of King Arthur. This was one of the three great "Matters" of the Western World. Spenser chose it for his poem; Ben Jonson said that Sidney had intended to use it; and Milton too had perhaps intended it. Had the Commonwealth succeeded as Milton desired, he might have written some sort of Arthuriad. Since the Commonwealth did not succeed, the only suitable Matter which remained was sacred history. Milton was not the first to treat of it; it had already been attempted and it was critically respectable. Poets who had tried it were Tasso, Du Bartas and Abraham Cowley, as well as some Christian Latin poets. The Matter could include both Biblical history and the Biblical account of the Creation.

Choosing sacred history presented both difficulties and advantages. The advantages were that Biblical history was just as suitable as classical myth for the purpose of teaching morality, or for ornamentation, or for dealing with marvellous events — the sun which stood still in the valley of Ajalon for Joshua was quite as good as anything that occurs in the *Metamorphoses,* never mind Homer or Virgil. It was already thought, too, that classical material was practically exhausted for poetical purposes.

The difficulty was that sacred history was not the only material available from the Bible. Christianity, which after all is not the primary material of the Old Testament, depends upon a theology which is fundamentally Greek as an intellectual structure: it was first Platonic, among the early Fathers, and subsequently Aristotelian. The matter of theology, too, to put it mildly, was not something temporal. So the problem for a poet became quite complex. It was possible to write sacred history, showing how the actions of God intervened, or could be discerned, in human events. (This had already been seen in the Old Testament where the Jews were conscious of being a race apart, and their history was a record of just such interventions). It had, too, already been attempted by Dryden, whose *Annus Mirabilis* was a short heroic poem, but one unfortunately liable to near-burlesque effects — as you can see from his description of the Great Fire, when the angels kept the flames from the naval magazines.

Secondly, it's very hard to write heroic poetry — that is to say, poetry about heroic action which requires chronological sequences — if you admit within your poem the Persons of the Trinity, who are, strictly speaking, outside time. In a poem like *Paradise Regained* this doesn't matter because the Christ of *Paradise Regained* appears as a human figure. The difficulty had already been found within the language of theology. There was one early heresy which was attacked precisely because it implied that since the Son was begotten, there must have been some point at which the Son had no existence: He wasn't co-eternal with the Father. That problem is one which occurs several times in *Paradise Lost* under different guises.

There are, however, further advantages, given Milton's choice of a Biblical subject. First, the ordinary heroic poem deals with the hero of one nation; but the Biblical heroic poem, using historic matter, deals with "typical" material, not national material, and hence is available, in theory at any rate, to any Christian nation. If you push back your subject to the Creation of man, you have, in effect, written the arch-heroic poem. You've dealt with the hero not of a nation but of the whole human race: someone who does not belong to any one racial group. Adam is Man. (This leads to certain basic structural devices in *Paradise Lost*).

There is still a further advantage. Your poem, although you couldn't necessarily know it, becomes much more available to a later time, to an age which is likely to see the story of Adam's fall as an attempt at an explanation and not as literal history. All the same, when I spoke of pushing your subject back to the Creation of Man I was being misleading, because it is not back to the Creation but to the Fall. That raises more problems for Milton, analogous to those of presenting the acts of God, which, of course, as he says are "immediate". The trouble is that there are basically two kinds of poem about the Divinity. A devotional poet, despite Samuel Johnson's objections, has no real difficulty: his matter is really his own fallen nature in some perceived relationship with the perfection of God. That is to say that although to define God's nature, and to realize God's nature in poetry, is impossible, it's not a problem you have to face in a devotional poem; you define the contrast between your nature and that of God. But Milton is dealing not with *fallen* man but with *falling* man. His story requires a sequence of action during which the Fall occurs. This risks a description of the nature of the Tree and of the fruit, and an explanation of why God should ever have forbidden the eating of the fruit. It involves, too, the question of whether the Fall occurred all at once or whether it was progressive, and if progressive, when it began, and so forth.

Milton so organizes his poem that as far as he can he shifts the emphasis away from this matter. For example, he deals with more than one fall; he deals with the consequences in history of Adam's fall; he tries to give the total context of the action of Adam and Eve; and he tries to dwell on the contrast of fallen and unfallen existence, both human and angelic, within the poem.

The risk still remains. The poem is bound to be built up, as any poem must be, of logical and counter-logical materials, if it's going to work at all.

XII

MILTON: *PARADISE REGAINED*

FRANK KERMODE

It's said of *Paradise Regained* that it's a poem, like *Samson Agonistes,* in which very little seems to be happening. I think the answer to that is very like the answer to *Samson Agonistes:* there's a lot happening if you know where to look. *Paradise Regained* used to be regarded as a direct sequel to *Paradise Lost* and that puzzled people because it doesn't seem to follow on from it an any way. You might expect it to be about redemption, perhaps, but is is not directly; it's about the conflict of Christ and Satan in the Wilderness, which was a necessary prelude to Christ's ministry. So there are obvious differences between this poem and *Paradise Lost.*

One of these differences, and perhaps the most important one at this very abstract level, is that the hero of *Paradise Regained* is not the first but the "second Adam"; unlike the first, he doesn't succumb to temptation but resists it and he here resists it in an exemplary way. The traditional commentaries on the Gospels which describe the Temptation in the Wilderness all try to make that Temptation typical of all other temptations; it includes every sort of temptation that there can be. They all say that Jesus in the wilderness had no divine support: he was pure *man,* and therefore we may and should imitate him in dealing with out temptations. Consequently, it's important for Milton to make this a total temptation. Here Marvell's *Dialogue Between the Resolved Soul and Created Pleasure* is very useful because it does in fact contain in microcosm the whole pattern of *Paradise Regained.* I'll come back to this later.

The question of whether, and how, you can call a poem the length of *Paradise Regained* an epic poem is not, I think, very important, but there are justifications for it. Milton recognized a type called the "brief epic." He described it in the *Reason of Church Government,* an early work of the 1640's, in which he wrote a biographical section which describes his ambitions. The model for the brief epic is the Book of Job which was read in this way, and, in fact, the structure and the general idea of *Paradise Regained* owe a great deal to the Book of Job; that's a "brief epic" as opposed to the diffuse epic written by, for example, Virgil or Tasso. The hero was a different kind of hero, a Christian hero, and therefore not in the least like say, Achilles in the *Iliad.*

The feeling that it was time to have an epic poem which was not about war, which didn't go in for old-style heroism, was quite strong in Milton's day. It was shared, for example, by his contemporaries, Cowley and Davenant, who believed that an epic poem should exhibit a "venerable and amiable image of heroic virtue" and this did not mean anything like the wrath of Achilles. It meant a willingness to suffer; the power to resist rather than to act. This idea is important for the second Book of the *Faerie Queene,* and in fact you'll find that the temptation of Guyon in the Cave of Mammon has many resemblances to the temptation of Christ in *Paradise Regained.* It was something of a stock theme. It had been treated before, notably by Giles Fletcher in the poem called *Christs Victorie and Triumph,* a very Spenserian poem, but one which has structural similarities to *Paradise Regained.*

I want to say a bit more about the kind of heroism involved in the poem. From St. Augustine on, there's a sense that the heroism of even the greatest Romans — Scipio Africanus, for example — was not a model for Christians, but only, as it were, a pagan *type* of Christian heroism, the reason being that to the pagan Romans the only reward of heroism was earthly honour, whereas the Christian's reward is not earthly at all. That is, broadly, the difference that Saint Augustine defines in *The City of God,* a book very much in Milton's mind here. If you take Christian heroism to be resistance and suffering rather than action, then, of course, the temptation of Christ in the wilderness must be seen in that way as a long series of negatives, as Christ says no to all that Satan can offer, whether they be temptations of the senses, wealth, glory, power, knowledge or whatever.

Milton gives the new heroic poem some of the old trappings by bringing in the councils of the gods, both heavenly and hellish; by giving it the "machinery" of the classical epic. But it is a paradoxical epic, nevertheless, since it is absolutely necessary that nothing should happen in it, except that Christ should continue to say no. That negativity creates difficulties that Milton was well aware of. You may remember that the opening lines of *Paradise Lost, Book IX,* touch on this subject. Milton compares his epic theme to that of Homer and argues that his epic theme is the greater theme, even though it isn't mainly about violent activity.

The version of the temptation scheme which Milton followed is basically that of St. Luke, Chapter 4, though it does occur also in the Gospels of Matthew and Mark. One has to remember that, to people of Milton's time, the text of the Bible was not just the words on the page. There was an extensive tradition of commentary and exegesis and it's extremely important to remember that every word was susceptible to being scrutinized in a very close way. So, when Luke described the temptations, he ends, in the Authorized Version, with these words:

13. And when the devil had ended all the temptation,
he departed from him for a season.

The word "all" is very important in the tradition because it was held to mean that the temptations which were brought to Jesus by the Devil in the wilderness were all the temptations there could possibly be. This was necessary for the idea that Jesus had withstood all possible temptations and that we could do the same. So, when you begin to set this out schematically and to introduce a great deal more, rather than simply saying "all" you have to specify, and that is what both Marvell in his short poem and Milton in his longer one do.

The theology of temptation used to be familiar and, I suppose, isn't familiar any more. We are more familiar with the Wildean theory — that we can resist anything except temptation. However, there was a general line on the subject. As Milton himself says, in his book on *Christian Doctrine,* there is good temptation whereby God tests people for the "righteous purpose of exercising or manifesting their faith and patience, as in the case of Job." Job is the great Old Testament personification of the tempted. This kind of temptation is therefore to be desired — "Blessed is the man who endureth temptation, for when he is tried he will receive the crown of life." In *Paradise Regained* Milton shows us what the crown of life is, because, as Jesus resists each of the temptations successively, he is gaining himself a better prize than anything he might have hoped for had he yielded to them. The same thing happens to Guyon in the Cave of Mammon, you remember; he rejects Philotime because he has another lady, a higher lady who represents not earthly honour but heavenly honour. (*Faerie Queene,* II. vii. 50).

Another favourite text that Milton used is from Hebrews:

For in that he himself hath suffered being tempted, he is able to succour them that are tempted.
(Chap. 2. v. 18

Again, it is very important that Jesus should win this victory over temptation
— called by Fletcher "the victory over sin" — so that he could go on to the
greater victory of death and crucifixion. In fact, the defeat of Satan is accom-
plished here, in the wilderness, by a man, not god; therefore it is a model for all
of us. Temptation is permissive; that is to say, Satan is allowed to tempt only
because God lets him do so. That is also true for Job. As Jesus says to Satan in
the wilderness:

Thy coming hither, though I know thy scope,
I bid not or forbid; do as thou find'st
Permission from above; thou can'st not more.

(I. 494-6)

The same thing is made very clear in the Book of Job, where Satan actually goes
and asks God for permission to tempt Job. The purpose of such temptation is to
refine the hero by suffering. The temptation of Job is to show that unaided man
can overcome his own temptations. Satan "might have learnt/Less overweening,
since he failed in Job" (I. 146, 147) says God in *Paradise Regained*. In fact there
are many references to the Book of Job. Satan says that God

Gave up into my hands Uzzean Job
To prove him, and illustrate his high worth;

(I. 369-70)

So the poem is very much about temptation, as indeed most of Milton's poems
are from *Comus* onwards. But here we have the archetype of temptation; one
which is the scheme for all the others and tells everybody else how to handle the
problem.

Milton is very concerned, also, to show that saying no is an heroic act; he
wants to make Jesus an heroic figure. This comes through very strongly in the
opening section of the poem, in the proposition and the first hundred lines or so.
The proposition is always worth close study. It's a formal part of the epic poem
and it's supposed to say in brief what the theme of the poem is:

I who erewhile the happy garden sung,
By one man's disobedience lost, now sing
Recovered Paradise to all mankind,
By one man's firm obedience fully tried
Through all temptations and the Tempter foiled
In all his wiles.

(I. 1-6)

Notice the word "all" there, it is strongly emphasised by repetition and so is the
contrast between the two men — "one man's disobedience" and then "one man's
firm obedience" — this is the contrast between the first and second Adam.

Then Milton follows, again traditionally, with an invocation to the Holy Spirit. More conventionally it is to a muse. What he wants is power "to tell of deeds/Above heroic, though in secret done"; they are "above heroic" though not in fact known to fame. And he finishes this preliminary material with the usual, and again wholly conventional, epic claim that what he is doing has never been done before:

> unrecorded left through many an age
> Worthy t'have not remained so long unsung.

(I. 16,17)

All Renaissance epic poetry alleged the same, so much so that the claim is classified as a *topos* in Curtius's book, *European Literature and the Latin Middle Ages.*

The poem then gets into the curious nature of Christ's heroism and the nature of this crisis in his life. He is about to begin his ministry and we hear something about his childhood and his mother. And we hear about the sort of heroism required of him in this initiatory episode. In it He will "first lay down the rudiments/Of his great warfare" (I. 157, 158). This is a necessary prelude to his mission. He will win a great victory, a conquest over Sin and Death, but this will not be a victory of arms, it will be a victory achieved "by humiliation and strong sufferance" (160). This is God speaking:

> first I mean
> To exercise him in the wilderness;
> There he shall first lay down the rudiments
> Of his great warfare, ere I send him forth
> To conquer Sin and Death, the two grand foes,
> By humiliation and strong sufferance:
> His weakness shall o'ercome Satanic strength.

(I. 155-61)

Weakness here means lack of arms, of course, not moral weakness; this "weakness" will overcome any of the blandishments that Satan can contrive and prepare him for his greater struggle. Here this exemplary, more than heroic virtue is represented as a kind of weakness, at any rate as non-violence. There is a great contrast, as I say, between Achilles and even Aeneas and Christ. But Milton has in mind, all the time, the ancient heroes and of course he uses them, not to show that Christ is like them but that He transcends them. Indeed, this is a characteristic of Renaissance fiction. Hercules was allegorized by the Neoplatonists to signify the extinction of desire by reason. There was a feeling that it was the ignorance of Christian doctrine that made ancient heroes glory in their wrath and strength, and that the Christian heroes had a different sort of heroi virtue and that it consisted in this extinction of appetite.

Milton refers back, from time to time, to Aeneas, when Jesus says:

> Therefore, above my years,
> The Law of God I read,

(I. 206, 207)

He is actually translating, with slight variations, a passage from the *Aeneid,* which tells how Aeneas took on manly responsibilities while he was still a boy. He refers back, more strikingly still, to when the angels say that his purpose in life is to "debel" (IV.605) the proud. I don't know whether that word occurs anywhere else but it is, of course, a literal translation of what must be the most famous line in the *Aeneid,* "*parcere subjectis et debellare superbos*" (*Aeneid,* 6.853), "to spare the conquered and overthrow the proud." The line describes the mission of Rome and when Milton uses the very unusual word "debel" he knows that everybody will remember Virgil's use of the verb *debellare.* He is not simply being clever.

People then, on the whole, didn't refer to Latin authors in order to show they knew them; they used them in order to make a point. The point here is to bring the context of the prophecy of the Empire into the poem, so that when Christ uses the word you will contrast that Empire which had to do with glory and possession and all the rest of it with Christ's new order, which has to do with the saving of the soul. You see that a lot can be done with a quote of that sort, and that is only one example of what goes on in *Paradise Regained;* there are many references from time to time to the *Aeneid,* and perhaps occasionally to Homer.

So, we have Christ poised at the beginning of this struggle, and this is another thing that is associated with heroism — the emergence from retirement into action — though this is a strange kind of inverted action, of course. Milton himself tended to see his own career in this light. He spent all those years at Horton preparing to burst on Europe (which was why Dr. Jonson made fun of him, saying he rushed back from Italy to be a hero in the Civil War but set up only as a schoolmaster, which didn't seem very grand). Nevertheless, there he was thinking of that same pattern of transition from contemplation into action when he wrote about Cromwell — in fact he writes about him exactly as if he were Jesus. Cromwell "grew up in the privacy of his own family and until his age was quite mature and settled, which he also passed in private, was chiefly known for his strict attendance upon the purer worship and for his integrity of life. He had cherished his confidence in God, he had nursed his great spirit in silence..." He excelled above all exercise "in the knowledge of himself; he had either destroyed or reduced to his own control all enemies within his own breast... He was 'commander first over himself.' To evince his extraordinary, his little less than divine, virtue, this mark will suffice; that there lived in him an energy whether of spirit and genius, or of discipline, established not by military rule only but by the rule of Christ and of sanctity."*

You can see how much that has in common with the account of Jesus emerging from the quiet of childhood when he nurses his great spirit in silence. This, incidentally, is the pattern Marvell adopts in the *Horatian Ode* when he speaks of Cromwell emerging from his private Gardens "where/He liv'd reserved and austere" and from which he could "by industrious Valour climbe" to a life of crisis and action. The formula is used, also, for Roman heroes who come from their farms to save the Republic; but they only saved the Republic, whereas Jesus saved mankind. In other words, Milton had a kind of heroic virtue and when he was praising that quality in himself, or in Cromwell, or in Fairfax, the other great Puritan leader, or in Jesus, he cast them into that mould. That was what heroic virtue was. So here he distinguishes between contemplation and action, and that is the beginning of the poem.

Jesus was born, he says, to "promote all truth" (205). His youth was spent in learning — "my mind was set/Serious to learn and know, and thence to do/What might be public good" (202-4). What he had to do was heroic acts. He first foresaw a military career, "To rescue Israel from the Roman yoke" (217) or to fight "Till truth were freed" (220), but that turns out to be a different matter from the sort of heroism that is required. His mother tells him to be cautious — "High are thy thoughts... above example high" (11.229 ff) but he must nourish them. So he waits — this idea of waiting is very important to Milton — and so "the time prefixed I waited" (269).

Then comes the announcement of the great shift from contemplation to action, at the time of the ministry of John the Baptist. Up till then his life had been of a kind that could hardly be more negative or inactive — "Private, unactive, calm" (II. 81). But now he sees "all his great works before him set." The faithful don't understand it, but he following the pattern of the emergence of the hero. The difference, of course, is that he emerges, as we find it described later, not to honour, but to trouble, not to action, but to suffering. Now that's the background to the beginning of the total temptation. If you look through the poem rapidly you'll see what form the total temptation takes.

First there's the temptation of the senses. This is done by means of the banquet. Actually the temptation of turning the stone into bread comes first, but that's from the Bible text and is a sort of preliminary to Milton's working out of the real structure of *Paradise Regained*. The temptation of the banquet belongs to the "topos" called the Banquet of Sense. That is, of course, what

---

* *Second Defence of the English People.* 1654.

Marvell is using in his poem. The Banquet topos deals not only with food but treats systematically all the senses.

Milton deals with the senses in the right order; that is to say, sight, hearing, smell (the middle sense, between sight and hearing, which work at a distance, and the two lowest senses, taste and touch, which depend on contact). The Banquet of Sense usually places the senses in that order, though to put hearing first was a permissible variant, as you see from Marvell's poem. Satan says "no interdict/Depends the touching of these viands pure" (II. 369-70). That is to say, he's assuring Jesus that there's nothing in the Jewish law that prevents him from partaking. However, Jesus, of course, rejects him — "To whom thus Jesus temperately replies" (II. 378). The adverbs used to introduce the replies of Jesus have always this kind of appropriateness. Here, "temperately" refers to Jesus' objective ability to assess the temptation. The eyes are tempted first, and then there's music and fragrance, and then the invitation to sit and eat and then, of course, the rejection and the carrying away of the banquet (404):

With sound of harpies' wings and talons heard.

That should remind you of the banquet in *The Tempest* (3.3.52) which Milton knew very well. In that play, as the men of sin are about to eat, the banquet is snatched away by Ariel dressed as a harpy. The harpy is an image of rapacity and uncontrolled sensual passion. In this guise Ariel makes his great speech "You are three men of sin" (3.3.53 seq.). This is all part of an elaborate *topos*.

Jesus's reason for rejecting the banquet is that he doesn't need it. It is rejected in order that he may gain a higher benefit, which is described in Book IV, 1.588 ff. This is a "table of celestial food. . . fetched from the Tree of Life." The heavenly banquet is given as a reward for resisting the earthly one.

Milton then goes on to another temptation. This is a very curious passage. If you look at Marvell's poem you will see that the next temptation after the systematic five senses is that of beauty, particularly sexual beauty. Milton obviously wanted to put this in, yet he couldn't really treat Jesus as if, like some later saints, he might have a particularly difficult time with this ordeal. Instead he puts it in the Council of Hell, and makes Belial, the "fleshliest" of all that fell, put up the proposal to the meeting — "Set women in his eye" (II. 153 ff) — and then he has a long passage in which Belial says how very charming women are and how much good they might do if the devils would only use them in this way. But, of course, Satan has got much more sense then to listen to Belial. He knows this would be a complete waste of time, and Belial's motion is rejected. The only reason you could possibly find for Milton having that passage in there at all is that he wants to stick to the same scheme as the one Marvell sets out so diagrammatically.

We pass on then to the next temptation, which is that of wealth. That, of course, is a temptation which Jesus has very little trouble resisting. And the next one, again in the right order, is the temptation of glory. This temptation turns on a distinction, which is quite clear in the text, between earthly and heavenly honour; the sort of honour available for a pagan and that which is available for the Christian. It is, clearly, one's standing with God that counts, not what other people say about you, and Jesus is very contemptuous of people's praise and indeed the "rabble" in general, whose opinion is not worth very much. But, of course, opinion has nothing to do with truth anyway; in heaven there's truth, on earth, opinion. This is a very ancient distinction and Milton here exploits it. The main issue is that the honour that goes with earthly success and praise is of no real interest to a Christian.

The next temptation is that of power. This is ostensibly a more serious temptation because it is part of Jesus's mission to liberate the Jews from the yoke of their conquerors, the Romans. However, He has no difficulty with that:

To whom our Saviour answered thus, unmoved. . .

(III. 386)

We then come to the beginning of Book IV, to a rather remarkable section in the poem where, still on the theme of political or military power, Milton introduces, in Satan's mouth, an example of another famous topos, *encomium urbis*. What happens, as you may know, in High Renaissance poetry, is that certain types or ways of doing things persist and one instance is the *encomium urbis* or praise of a city — usually a praise of Rome, the eternal city, the city which is, as it were, the mother of them all and which in fact first inspired this particular genre. So there are prescribed ways of expressing the praise of Rome. The central text is the VIth Book of the *Aeneid*, the prophetic book, which deals with the greatness of Rome, the *urbs aeterna*. The Roman Imperium is the first great climax of history. This was very important for Christians because the establishment of the Augustan peace coincided with the birth of Christ, and so the period of Augustan authority in the history of Rome was taken as a type of the history of Christianity; and, of course, the Roman Empire, converted to Christianity later on, made it possible to prescribe a universal religion.

The *encomium urbis* begins at line 44:

The city which thou seest no other deem

Than great and glorious Rome, queen of the earth. . .

Satan is showing Jesus, as he promised, the kingdoms of the earth. He goes on at some length in praise of Rome — "All nations now to Rome obedience pay" (80). The *encomium orbis* is a climax to the temptations of wealth, glory and power. Rome, unlike Parthia to which it is compared in Book III possesses not only military power but also civilization; it has "civility of manners, arts, and arms" (83). Satan offers Jesus the power of the Roman Emperor now that he has been shown "the kingdoms of the world, and all their glory" (89). But this is only the earthly city, not the heavenly city; it is the "*civitas terrena*" and not the "*civitas dei*" — the contrast derives from St. Augustine. And of course you must reject one before you gain the other: the Roman power must be rejected just as firmly as the oriental power of Persia. Jesus rejects both kingdoms and remembers the words of Daniel (2.34-35, 4.11) when he says there is another kingdom, not yet with us, the fifth kingdom, which will spread and overshadow all the earth:

Or as a stone that shall to pieces dash
All monarchies besides throughout the world.

(IV. 149-150)

This is a crucial rejection because it provokes what has been called the recognition of Satan. Satan realizes what he is up against and requests impudently that Jesus fall down and worship him. Jesus says "plain thou now appear'st/That Evil One" (194).

But we are not yet done with the temptations. We have still got the most difficult of them all to understand. Milton has dealt with the senses, wealth, glory, power, but he has not dealt with knowledge. In Marvell's poem forbidden knowledge is also the last, climactic temptation.

I haven't said much about the manner of the poem so I'll just interpose a word here. You must see that the blank verse is nearly always very different from that of *Paradise Lost*. It has a kind of limpidity, a kind of transparency, a lack of the elevation and the kind of excitement that *Paradise Lost* is noted for. It is very much a more difficult taste to acquire than *Paradise Lost*. So it's very striking that when we get to the temptation of learning we get what is, I think, by far the most moving section of the poem and, in a conventional sense, the most beautiful.

Satan invites Jesus to look down again from the "specular mount," not at Rome this time, but at Athens:

behold
Where on the Aegean shore a city stands
Built nobly, pure the air, and light the soil,
Athens, the eye of Greece, mother of arts
And eloquence, native to famous wits
Or hospitable, in her sweet recess,
City or suburban, studious walks and shades;

(IV. 237-43)

They see Plato's academy, the "olive grove of academe"; then Aristotle, he "who bred/Great Alexander to subdue the world" (252). And finally, and most poignantly, the one person who could be called a pagan type of Christ, Socrates:

> To sage philosophy next lend thine ear,
> From heaven descended to the low-roofed house
> Of Socrates — see there his tenement —
> Whom well inspired the oracle pronounced
> Wisest of men. . .

(IV. 272-76)

And so on to later schocls of philosophy. But, at line 285, Jesus replies:

> Our Saviour sagely thus replied:

"sagely" because his wisdom is clearly superior to the wisdom of these philosophers. His reply is very destructive. He attacks all philosophy and poetry that isn't in Hebrew and the reason he does this is made clear right at the beginning:

> Think not but that I know these things, or think
> I know them not; not therefore am I short
> Of knowing what I ought. He who receives
> Light from above, from the Fountain of Light,
> No other doctrine needs, though granted true;
> But these are false, or little else but dreams. . .

(IV. 286-91)

People argue about nature and about the world, but all this knowledge is really totally irrelevant because the only knowledge necessary to salvation is the knowledge that God himself imparts.

Now, it may seem very strange that so learned a man as Milton, a man so dedicated to ancient poetry and philosophy, should make it exemplary that one should pay no attention to such learning. In fact the sin of curiosity, Donne's sin — *curiositas* — concerns not simply forbidden knowledge but also unnecessary knowledge. "Some seek knowledge merely but to know" as Greville said, "and idle curiosity that is." You mustn't seek knowledge merely because it is *interesting*; you must seek it positively and exclusively as an aid to the salvation of your soul. If you take a very extreme puritan view on this it doesn't leave you anything to read, really, except the Bible.

However, other people drew the line more liberally. This was a constant preoccupation in the Renaissance and was discussed again and again. In fact the controversy goes back, once more, to Saint Augustine. Milton is not speaking here for himself. He's taking the hardest possible line when he says "He who receives/Light from above, from the Fountain of Light/No other doctrine needs, though granted true." Even if ancient learning is seen to be true, you still have to reject it, you still don't need it. But it isn't always true. You will remember that in *Paradise Lost* Milton is constantly bringing in ancient mythology, in order to have it in, but then saying it's not true. Milton was himself, I think, in a difficult position here and there is great tension in this section which has perhaps been lacking in the rest of the poem. But the *doctrine* is clear enough; all unholy learning is unnecessary; and in fact, compared to true learning, even the finest discoverers of secular learning are like "children gathering pebbles on the shore" (330).

Then he goes on to ask why we should need the Greek poets, we have the Hebrew poets. He writes about the poetry of the Old Testament, particularly the Psalms, of course:

>   All our law and story strewed
> With hymns, our Psalms with artful terms inscribed,
> Our Hebrew songs and harps in Babylon,

(IV. 334-6)

These suit Christians much better then Greek poetry, and he is probably thinking of Pindar when he talks about "swelling epithets"

>   thick laid
> As varnish on a harlots cheek, the rest,
> Thin sown with aught of profit or delight,
> Will far be found unworthy to compare
> With Sion's songs, to all true tastes excelling,
> Where God is praised aright. . .

(IV. 343-8)

(That is really quite a conventional statement of the superiority of Hebrew over Greek poetry — although at this time the principles of Hebrew poetry were not at all understood.)

In the same way the whole of Greek philosophy is rejected. Many books are "wearisome' — that is itself a quotation from the Bible (Eccles: 12.12):

>   who reads
> Incessantly, and to his reading brings not
> A spirit and judgement equal or superior
> (And what he brings, what needs he elsewhere seek?)
> Uncertain and unsettled still remains,
> Deep versed in books and shallow in himself,

(IV. 322-7)

That's the final, conventional rejection of useless human learning with the allegation that it can be a great evil: at best it is useless, at worst it is destructive. What you need for salvation is the spirit within you and nothing else, you certainly don't need these poets. As far back as the *Reason of Church Government,* Milton has been saying things like this: "Pindarus and Callimachus are in most things worthy, but those frequent songs throughout the law and prophets are beyond all these, not in their divine argument alone, but in the very critical art of composition." That is to say, in his earlier days — 1643 — Milton was willing to let people read Pindar, but he wanted them to see that David was a better poet.

However you read that — and it's probably the most interesting temptation in the poem — it does complete the pattern as laid down for the temptations. After the rejection of learning Marvell, you remember, says:

Triumph, triumph, victorious Soul;

The World has not one pleasure more.

So when Satan adds learning to all other temptations the pattern is finished. One resource only is left to Satan, a temptation executed by violence. In Elizabeth Pope's book on *Paradise Lost, Paradise Regained and The Tradition,* you'll find an argument that all Milton's temptations had a triple form — necessity, force and fraud. I don't think this works for *Paradise Regained;* however you can read her book and judge for yourselves. (The other important, vast book on *Paradise Regained* is by Barbara Lewalski and it is called *Milton's Brief Epic*). However, when all the temptations are done there is this temptation of violence. Christ is swept up to the pinnacle of the Temple of Jerusalem. This, of course, is in the Bible. Jesus must throw himself off and trust to the Angels to lift him up. Well, as He has triumphed by doing absolutely nothing all the way through, He is surely not going to change now, so we get a very memorable line as the climax of the poem. When Satan tempts him to fall off the Temple, Jesus says:

"Tempt not the Lord thy God', he said, and stood.

(561)

This is a remarkable Miltonic line. The heroic action here might seem to be to throw yourself off, but in fact to stand is the right thing to do — the opposite of action.

That is the end of the temptations. All that remains is for Christ to receive angelic succour, just like Guyon at the end of his ordeal in the Cave of Mammon, and to go home — He "Home to his mother's house private returned" (639). That is a famous and strange last line for an epic poem. It fades into the quiet which has really been the mood of the poem all through, and yet within that quiet great heroic feats are supposed to have been achieved. That was the difficulty Milton faced. Whether you think he has succeeded in bringing it off, and showing true heroic virtue in the figure of a man who does nothing but resist all the temptations, remains for you to decide. You see what a very difficult choice of subject it was for an epic poem; how much less it gave Milton than *Paradise Lost* with all its encyclopaedic scope. Certainly it's a poem of very high interest. There's an immense intellectual pressure at work in trying to get everything right in so strange and important a theme.

XIII

MILTON: *SAMSON AGONISTES*

FRANK KERMODE

If you've been looking at W.R. Parker's biography of Milton, which is the standard biography now, or at Carey and Fowler's annotated edition, which is the best edition to use, you'll have seen that both these authorities regard *Samson Agonistes* as an early poem of Milton's, belonging to the late 1640's. I don't believe that. However, we had better give a second's consideration to these arguments about its being an early poem. I think they largely amount to an ability on the part of these scholars to show that there's no internal evidence for it being a *late* poem. Someone said it was late fairly late in the tradition, in the eighteenth century, and this was largely assumed to be the case until a few years ago when Parker pointed out that, curiously, it was never mentioned in early biographies of Milton as being a late work, and that in any case Milton must have been very busy writing *Paradise Regained* at the time when he was supposed to be writing *Samson Agonistes*.

One answer to that argument is that we don't have a day to day account of what Milton was doing in those last years. It's quite possible that *Samson Agonistes* was planned much earlier than it was written. We know from what Milton says about tragedy in the *Reason of Church Government,* and from the ideas for tragedy that he wrote in the Trinity Manuscript, that he had been thinking about Samson very much earlier, so it's quite plausible that he thought of Samson, along with a great many other possible subjects, in his youth. But that he wrote the tragedy early seems to me quite inconceivable. It's one of the most daring experimental works, if you see it right, in English verse. It has the most astonishing prosodic variations, and common sense, I think, dictates the old view that he would have written *Paradise Lost,* with that immense development of straightforward blank verse, before he wrote this work which departs so often from the canons of blank verse.

One difficulty, of course, is that in the prefatory note to *Paradise Lost* Milton attacks rhyme. He says he doesn't care for rhyme, which is a modern bondage with which the ancients weren't bothered and, of course, he doesn't use it in *Paradise Lost* except for very special effects. But he does use it in *Samson Agonistes* and it's rather curious that he should have written against rhyme and then just a very few years later used it extensively. But I think there are reasons for not letting that sway us. One reason is that Milton was anxious to justify what was, after all, a very remarkable thing to do — to write a long, non-dramatic poem in blank verse. He was defending *Paradise Lost* in that note. Another reason is that he had the idea (wrongly as we now know, because Hebrew prosody was not at all understood in Milton's lifetime) that there were some rhymes and half-rhymes in the Psalms and therefore he thought that he could get that Old Testament poetry feeling, if you like, by using rhymes, in a very irregular way, in *Samson Agonistes.*

I won't go into all the details of this argument; there are many contributing details. One is that The Argument of *Samson Agonistes* is not an accurate reflection of what happens in it. In a way that's true. There's no mention of Dalila and there's no mention of Harapha in The Argument, and as they are two of the principal characters that is rather strange. Manoa is somewhat mis-leadingly represented; he is a bit of a nag as well as a comfort to Samson, though in The Argument he's just called comforting. It is rather curious that, having just written a tragedy, you shouldn't then be able to write a decent paraphrase of it, but it's susceptible to explanation. Someone else might have written it or it might have been written in haste. There are all sorts of possibilities, but it does not mean, I think, that there must have been an earlier version without these characters in it.

I shan't say any more about this except to repeat, perhaps wrongly, that it seems to me out of the question that *Samson Agonistes* was an early work. It belongs very much to Milton's old age, I would have thought. I do not believe we should make too much of the personal parallel between Samson and Milton, but it is very strong if you think of it as a late work. They are both blind. They both served their country in what they took to be heroic ways. They have both fallen on evil times. None of that applies, of course, to the earlier Milton. You can attach as little or as much importance to that as you like. Also, of course, the early biographies of Milton, including those of his nephew, Phillips, are unreliable in other ways, so one needn't be too disturbed by the failure to mention one of his works.

It's clear that *Samson Agonistes* is, in a sense, a last Renaissance tribute to antiquity before something else, called neo-classicism, takes over. Here we have a Renaissance play which is very closely modelled on Greek tragedy and which is, nevertheless, Christianized. There are two traditional debates about *Samson Agonistes* — one is whether it's more Heleenic than Hebraic and the other is whether it's a bore because nothing happens in it. I think the answer to the first point — as Milton makes clear in his preface to the work — is that he is not slavishly imitating classical Greek tragedy; he is giving it an Hebraic-Christian quality and adapting the Greek form so that it can bear it. He points out the differences between his work and Greek tragedy: for example, it is not sung and, more important, it isn't acted; it's a closet drama, if you like. And it would be inconceivable for Milton, much as he admired Sophocles, to reproduce Sophocles' world view. Milton was a Christian and his hero was an Old Testament prophet. The end of *Oedipus Rex,* with the Chorus saying it would be best not to be born at all, is really inconceivable for Milton. His end, of course, was affirmation of divine justice and also of the secure and powerful place that the elect play in the operation of providence. So that you don't get the mood of Greek tragedy, though in many ways the play follows the structure and movement of Greek tragedy. There's a whole book devoted to that by W.R. Parker, called *Milton's Debt to Greek Tragedy in Samson Agonistes.*

Milton, incidentally, still has a certain celebrity for having introduced an emendation into a play of Euripides which stuck. He was quite a good scholar in the conventional sense. He draws on each one of the major three tragedians — on Aeschylus, because there are certain similarities between Milton's play and the *Prometheus Bound:* on Euripides, particularly in the passages dealing with the physical pain and torment; but, most of all, on Sophocles. The Greek play which is most like *Samson Agonistes* in theme, I suppose, is *Oedipus at Colonus,* the last of the Oedipus plays and the one that has a blind hero. There's another more important borrowing from Sophocles, which I'll be talking about in some detail, though in other terms, namely his use of the famous device of Sophoclean irony. This is the irony that takes effect when there is a gap between what *you* know about the outcome and what the characters know about the outcome. That is to say that the characters are talking on the basis of incomplete knowledge, whereas your knowledge is more complete. It lends itself to all kinds of subtle effects and to Milton it was related to the whole question of how man can interrogate the providence of God. God, of course, is fully aware of the end of the action and man is not.

This leads us into the main traditional conflict of Samson criticism: is it a bore? The great exponent of that view is Dr. Johnson, but even in his own time he was quite often sensibly confuted on this point and, unless you expect Samson to rush around with the jawbone of an ass on stage or have a Cecil B. de Mille scene of a temple collapsing, it really is rather absurd to say that nothing happens in this play. However, I thought it would be useful to set out diagramatically the things that do happen in the play and the way they contribute to one another.

	1 Samson's Destiny	2 Motivation	3 "Unwisely" marries	4 Quality of wife	5 Ultimate Result
(A)	Born "for some great act"	"Intimate impulse"	Woman of Timna	Bad	Good (Death to Philistines)
(B)	– ditto –	– ditto –	Dalila	– ditto –	– ditto –

N.B. At the time of action B5 is not known so B2 is not understood.

We must think first of the promises made by God to Samson:

Samson is born "for some great act" – he is announced as "separate to God". In spite of these promises Samson has been struck low. He's "Eyeless in Gaza at the mill with slaves." We begin to get some explanation of how this happened. The first reason, stated with great emphasis, is his marriage to the woman of Timna. This wife never appears, but marriage becomes a very important theme in the play. It was a strange marriage for Samson, a Nazarite, to make, for she was a Philistine – therefore Samson broke the law. The woman, of course, turned out to be bad, but the outcome was, curiously enough, good, because it was as a direct consequence of her infidelity that a large number of Philistines got killed. His motive for marrying the woman of Timna was – and this is the key phrase – that he had an "intimate impulse"; that's to say he felt a very powerful inner prompting to marry her. This can be set out, crudely, in the following way:

				Woman	outcome
"Intimate impulse"	– marriage (1) –	to woman of Timna	– broke the law	– Bad	– good

His second marriage is to Dalila. Dalila is also Philistine, so when he married her he again broke the law. This woman turns out to be *really* bad. But this brings us up to date and the outcome also seems to be bad; Samson is "Eyeless in Gaza at the mill with slaves." Samson says his only excuse for having done what he did is that he had an "intimate impulse." He had argued with himself, on the analogy of his first marriage, that things would go well, but now, says Samson, it's perfectly clear from the way that things have gone that this is not so. So a developing parallel seems to go wrong at the end.

				women	outcome
"Intimate impulse" —	marriage (2) —	to Dalila —	broke the law —	bad —	bad

Now, remember what I was saying about Sophoclean irony. Samson, Manoa, the Chorus are all arguing on the basis of an action which they think is complete, but which is not complete. That's a simple formula for what is happening at the level of plot in *Samson Agonistes*.

This takes us into the time of the play. All that I have described so far is supposed to have happened in the past. After a lot of talk about it, Dalila comes in and then Harapha. This stirs Samson up and he gets excited. Then the Officer comes in and tells Samson he must come with him to perform at Dagon's feast. Samson replies:

Shall I abuse this consecrated gift
Of strength, again returning with my hair,
After my great transgression, so requite
Favor renewd, and add a greater sin
By prostituting holy things to idols;
A Nazarite in place abominable?

11. 1354-9

In other words, the invitation to the games is declined because it would mean breaking the law. The Officer leaves and something peculiar happens within Samson — he changes his mind:

Be of good courage, I begin to feel
Some rousing motions in me which dispose
To something extraordinary my thoughts
I with this messenger will go along. . .

11. 1381-4

He says that he will do nothing to stain his vow as a Nazarite, but, as he has just said the act of going would do that, we are getting the same pattern again. The outcome, however, is good because Samson brings the Temple down.

	outcome
"intimate impulse" – invitation to games – broke the law –	good

Thus, with the action complete, we see that the last sequence revises that bases on Samson's marriage to Dalila, to make it run parallel to the first. The outcome of the second marriage turns out to be good.

		women	outcome
1."Intimate impulse" – marriage (1) – woman of Timna	– broke the law	– bad –	good
2."Intimate impulse" – marriage (2) – Dalila	–broke the law	– bad –	(bad) good
3."Intimate impulse" – invitation to games	–broke the law		good

Now, the point of all this is that Samson is "separate to God." He is one of the elect. The elect were, of course, the saints, and Samson, as an Old Testament figure cannot be a saint, but there's no difficulty about that. The typological reading of the Old Testament could very well have Samson standing for one of God's elect in the full Christian sense.

The question naturally arises as to why Samson had to go through all of this and that is what the play is continually asking: Does God preserve the elect? Secondly, if God has let Samson fall, as he has done, into dishonour and slavery, *why* has He done this? Various explanations have been put forward – that Samson is an exemplary figure, turning on the wheel of fortune, or that it's a warning against trusting women. These are traditional views. People say of the famous misogynist Chorus in *Samson Agonistes* that it shows how much Milton disliked women. That Chorus has the same status as the Chorus which says God has deserted Samson. It's not true. The time to go into what Milton really thought about women is when one is talking about *Paradise Lost*, and particularly about Books IV and IX. On the whole, I think, his writings show that Milton was quite fond of women and placed a good deal of value on sexual pleasure.

But that's not what we're discussing now. We're concerned with the inadequate attempts of the people within the play to explain how it came about that Samson had been deserted by God and allowed by Him to fall into this state. Is Samson to blame? The official answer is yes, but the play does seem to say, in various ways, that, nevertheless, God does seem to be very contrarious. "God of our fathers, what is man?" – in that Chorus the word "contrarious" is actually used of God. He does treat his chosen very strangely indeed. Milton has to submerge this in a kind of terrific confidence that in the end the suffering of the elect can be part of God's mysterious way of working things out. He made the laws and He can break them; the Chorus says this quite specifically. The law exists as an *instrument* of God; when it serves His purposes it can be broken and this is what happens three times if you include the case of Dagon's feast.

Now, if you admit this as the general course of the play, then I think that the contention that nothing happens in it becomes absurd and irrelevant. Let me go roughly through the play and show this.

First there's a prologue of a roughly Euripidean kind in which we're told, very effectively, about Samson's blindness and about his being at the mill, and the contrast between this and all that was foretold by heaven. The prophecy that accompanied his birth has been denied:

O wherefore was my birth from Heaven foretold
Twice by an angel. . . .?

11. 23,4

Then we hear of his being "separate to God" and of his present condition:

Lower than bondslave! Promise was that I
Should Israel from Philistian yoke deliver;
Ask for this great deliverer now, and find him
Eyeless in Gaza at the mill with slaves.

11. 38-41

(This is a very famous line, partly because it has two or possibly even three caesuras.) And then immediately we have the cry that goes up often in the play:

Yet stay, let me not rashly call in doubt
Divine prediction. . .

11. 43,4

And that is what we're not supposed to do also. We have, already, a kind of confidence that the divine prediction will be fulfilled.

Then he explains how he lost his strength by talking too much, by telling his Philistian wife the source of his strength — his "capital secret" as he calls it later, with one of these heavy miltonic puns. There's some moralizing as well:

God, when he gave me strength, to show withal
How slight the gift was, hung it in my hair.

11. 58,9

and then, again:

But peace! I must not quarrel with the will
Of highest dispensation.

11. 60,1

Again he says that. And one of the things that makes the poem moving is that there is a sense of human outrage at the degree of suffering inflicted and a difficulty in reconciling it with a notion of a benevolent God. It gives real tension to the verse.

Samson turns straight from that into a complaint about his lost sight and to the beautiful ode which is the first indication we have of the tremendous prosodic variety in the poem:

O dark, dark, dark, amid the blaze of noon,
Irrecoverably dark, total eclipse
Without all hope of day!

ll. 80-2

There are two famous works which deal with the verse of *Samson Agonistes.* One is by Robert Bridges and it is somewhat superseded now; another is an excellent book by F.T. Prince, called *The Italian Element in Milton's Verse,* in which you can see that Milton got his scheme from the Italian *canzoni,* with their irregular length of line and their irregular rhyming. Prince discusses this in detail. What we get here, of course, goes beyond that, into a sort of free verse with quite extraordinary power. At last we feel liberated after all the blank verse of *Paradise Lost* and the four books of *Paradise Regained* with all its variety and syntactical power. We are suddenly into something quite new. This is why I find it quite incredible that the whole thing was written long before *Paradise Lost* and just after *Lycidas.*

This is another famous "Euripidean" passage; the complaint that sight should be confined to the eyes while feeling is diffused throughout the body has extraordinary force:

why was the sight
To such a tender ball as th'eye confined?
So obvious and so easy to be quenched,
And not, as feeling, through all parts diffused,
That she might look at will through every pore?

ll. 93-7

"Obvious" is a beautiful latinism here, meaning both easily seen, and so open, so easily got at.

The ode is interrupted by the Chorus. Now, Milton certainly believed in the Chorus and justified his use of it. (Remember that French neo-classicism had dispensed with the Chorus by this time.) Milton didn't know as much about the use of the Greek Chorus as is now known, but he saw a use for it, and used it with good effect.

The first explanation the Chorus gives, having said what a splendid hero Samson used to be when he slew people with the jawbone of an ass, or tore up the gates of Gaza, is that other people must be given an example, a lesson. They use the image of a mirror. This was used, as in the *Mirror for Magistrates,* to mean an example, something to which we should look to see our state reflected, and learn from that:

O mirror of our fickle state,
Since man on earth unparalleled!
The rarer thy example stands,
By how much from the top of wondrous glory
Strongest of mortal man,
To lowest pitch of abject fortune thou art fall'n. . .

11. 164-9

They put forward the explanation that Samson is one more in a long tradition of fallen, illustrious men. I expect you know all about this but I shall briefly repeat it. There is a whole tradition, going back to the Middle Ages, of *De Casibus* literature. That simply means stories about the falls of great men, or even women sometimes. They came into English in the sixteenth century, notably in the collection of poems called the *Mirror for Magistrates.* The magistrates look into this book and see what they must not do if they are to avoid retribution or a fall from pride. What the Chorus is doing here, then, is simply treating Samson as another instance of the *De Casibus* theme.

There's a book which I might mention, though I think it is mostly wrong, by a man called F.M. Krouse, called *Milton's Samson and the Christian Tradition.* He goes through all the things that were said about Samson in commentaries on the Bible and the rest of it. There were several dominant things that interested people about Samson. One was whether or not he committed suicide. St. Augustine, in the *City of God,* goes into a long discussion of whether a Christian might ever commit suicide. It was a real problem in Augustine's day when a religious woman might face the question of whether, if she is about to be raped by a heretic, she might take her own life. Augustine says no, but he does in the course of his argument discuss some famous suicides; Lucretia is one and Samson is another. Of course he says that Samson didn't really commit suicide at all. Anyway, Krouse discusses the exemplary quality of Samson from all sorts of different angles like that. Not particularly usefully, I think, because Milton doesn't seem to have had a lot of time for most of them. But he does use the *De Casibus* theme and he does allude, in passing, to the question of suicide.

The Chorus and Samson then have a debate. Samson laments having divulged the gift of God to a sinful woman. The Chorus corrects him:

Tax not divine disposal; wisest men
Have erred, and by bad women been deceived;

And shall again, pretend they ne'er so wise.

11. 210-2

The play is hardly begun and we're already talking about women and marriage. This is really basic.

Samson starts telling of the woman of Timna, his first wife. She was "the daughter of an infidel." His parents blamed him, but

> they knew not
> That what I motioned was of God; I knew
> From intimate impulse, and therefore urged
> The Marriage on. . .

11. 221-4

He is very positive about that. Even at this low point in his life he knows that that first marriage was right. He then continues:

> and therefore urged
> The Marriage on; that by occasion hence
> I might begin Israel's deliverance,
> The work to which I was divinely called.
> She proving false, the next I took to wife
> (O that I never had! fond wish too late!)
> Was in the vale of Sorec, Dalila,
> That specious monster, my accomplished snare.

Notice particularly the next lines:

> I thought it lawful from my former act,
> And the same end, still watching to oppress
> Israel's oppressors.

11. 224-33

Now he wrongly assumes that the analogous "intimate impulse" prompting him to marry Dalila was false. But, of course, this is the kind of irony that comes from an action not being completed. We see later on that he was right to think it lawful; that the analogy was, in fact, an exact one.

The Chorus then reminds him rather bitterly that although Samson had been active in its defence, "yet Israel still serves." Samson then begins an extraordinary attack on the Israel Government, saying that is their fault and not his. Here, again, I think it's hard to avoid the feeling that Milton is really talking about the failure of the Revolution, the collapse of the Commonwealth. It is hard to avoid the idea that in a certain sense Milton's position was a bit like Samson's.

The Chorus beginning:

> Just are the ways of God,

And justifiable to men;

1. 293 ff.

is a famous one. The dogged confidence that it expresses helps us to feel that this is so. This confidence is extended even to Samson's marriage:

He would not else, who never wanted means,
Nor in respect of the enemy just cause,
To set his people free,
Have prompted this heroic Nazarite,
Against his vow of strictest purity
To seek in marriage that fallacious bride,
Unclean, unchaste.

11 315-21

They admit that there was a reason why Samson sought in marriage the woman of Timna, but that the reason was hidden from them:

Down, Reason, then, at least vain reasonings down. . .

Then Manoa, Samson's father arrives. It may seem that Milton is taking us over the same ground again here, but actually the poem hasn't been going on for very long and we do need to have stressed very strongly the contrast between the great hero, "separate to God," and this miserable figure, this slave of the Philistines. We have got to get the feeling of being at the end of the action. It seems that Milton succeeded only too well in this and that is why people think that nothing happens. There's a false end, as it were, when there seems to be nothing left to do but moan about it.

Manoa rubs it in:

I cannot praise thy marriage choices, son,
Rather approved them not; but thou did'st plead
Divine impulsion prompting how thou might'st
Find some occasion to infest our foes.

11. 420-3

In reply to this Samson concludes with a sort of blank assertion of confidence in God:

This only hope relieves me, that the strife
With me hath end; all the contest is now
'Twixt God and Dagon. . .

1. 460-2

That's one of those remarks which we know to be both true and false. True because the strife is between God and Dagon, but untrue in that Samson is wrong in thinking he will have no part in it. Manoa wonders what can be done to ease the plight of Samson and, like everyone else, assumes that Samson from now on is not going to have any more part in the action. They lament this; they lament the fact that he is a temperate man and yet gives way to these impulses of passion which have led him to decay, and that he should be in the ironical position of having all this strength and yet not be in a position to use it. Again, Milton scores with all these ironies.

Samson has another Euripidean lament on torment:

O that torment should not be confined
To the body's wounds and sores,

1. 606ff.

The imagery is taken from disease:

 wounds immedicable
Rankle, and fester, and gangrene,
To black mortification.

All of this leads the Chorus to the outburst which I have already mentioned:

God of our fathers, what is man!
That thou towards him with hand so various —
Or might I say contrarious? —
Temper'st thy providence through his short course,

1. 667ff

The Chorus is not talking about ordinary men:

But such as thou hast solemnly elected.

That's the real point; why does God use his heroes as he does? Well, we've learnt half of the lesson and we're now going to be told that the suffering Samson is, in some mysterious way, part of God's plan for him and for Israel. I won't spend time now on the Dalila scene. Some people think she comes rather well out of this. William Empson's book, *Milton's God,* has a chapter on that scene. He rather perversely argues that she wins and that Milton was really on the other side of the argument rather than the one he pretends to be on. You can work that one out for yourselves.

It is after he gets cross with Dalila and Harapha that Samson begins to revive. The Chorus celebrates this with an ode:

Oh how comely it is and how reviving
To the spirits of just men long oppressed,
When God into the hands of their deliverer
Puts invincible might. . .

11. 1268-71

But, they go on to say, this is not Samson's case. Patience is often what the saints have to show; there are active saints and patient saints. Some have to suffer and some have to act. Samson is now one of the sufferers.

Then comes the crucial incident, the hinge of the whole play, the rejection of the Officer's invitation. And then, without obvious motivation, its acceptance. Then follows the climax; the messenger's account of what Samson did. The play claims the full justification of God and the way in which he treats his heroes, his elect. It involves that effect of Greek tragedy which Milton valued very much, as he explained at the beginning, namely the catharsis, the purgation, which he understood in the medical sense. There is a purgation of the passions of pity and terror. He emphasizes in the semi-chorus at the end, the purgative forces of Samson's suffering as well as the victory of the God of Israel over his enemies.

The important chorus, from the point of view of Milton's idea of heroism, is that beginning at line 1687; this gives us a very beautiful figure, an image of how God treats his elect:

But he, though blind of sight,
Despised and thought extinguished quite,
With inward eyes illuminated,
His fiery virtue roused
From under ashes into sudden flame,
And an an ev'ning dragon came,
Assailant on the perchèd roosts
And nests in order ranged
Of tame villatic fowl; but as an eagle
His cloudless thunder bolted on their heads.

Then comes the famous image of the phoenix, a traditional emblem of regeneration, here applied particularly to the elect of God:

So virtue, giv'n for lost,
Depressed, and overthrown, as seemed,
Like that self-begotten bird
In the Arabian woods embost,
That no second knows no third,
And lay erewhile a holocaust,
From out her ashy womb now teemed,
Revives, reflourishes, then vigorous most
When most unactive deemed,
And though her body die, her fame survives,
A secular bird, ages of lives.

"vigorous most/When most unactive deemed" figures the hero who seems to have lost his powers and to be inactive, but who is still "separate to God" and still his instrument.

Finally, the closing chorus has a deliberate treatment of the theme of catharsis, together with the notion of God's champion as, at times, apparently separate from God and yet always under his care:

All is best, though we oft doubt,
What th'unsearchable dispose
Of Highest Wisdom brings about,
And ever best found in the close.

ll. 1745 ff

You have to wait for the close before you can see the point of all that has gone gone before:

Oft he seems to hide his face,
(again this contrarious aspect of God)
But unexpectedly returns
And to his faithful champion hath in place
Bore witness gloriously;
. . .
His servants he, with new acquist
Of true experience from this great event,
With peace and consolation hath dismissed,
And calm of mind, all passion spent.

It was not up to the Greek tragedians to quote Aristotle because he came afterwards, but Milton did and closes his play with a reference to Aristotle's *Poetics* and the idea of catharsis. This was possible because the plot of the play so accurately reflects the tension between notions of divine providence and the experience of suffering. The triumph may seem a bit barbarous, but it reconciles the mind to the humiliation of living and dying. Hence the catharsis.